WIDE MY WORLD NARROW MY BED

WIDE MY WORLD NARROW MY BED

Luci Swindoll

MULTNOMAH
Portland, Oregon 97266

Cover design and illustration: Paul Lewis

© 1982 by Multnomah Press
Printed in the United States of America

Library of Congress Cataloging in Publication Data
Swindoll, Luci, 1932-
    Wide my world, narrow my bed.

    1. Single people—Conduct of life.   2. Swindoll, Luci, 1932-
I. Title.
HQ800.S86   1982   305'.90652   82-7890
                                                   AACR2
ISBN 0-88070-004-1
ISBN 0-930014-89-8 (pbk.)

                90   91   92   —   10   9   8   7   6   5   4

*This book is written as a tribute
to my father,*

EARL SWINDOLL

*who died March 26, 1980, at the age of eighty-seven.
By his constant loving compassion for me during
childhood, and by his support and encouragement
of me as a single adult, I have a heart that is full of
gratitude for the richness of life. For that, no daughter
could have loved or appreciated her father more
than I.*

Contents

Luci Swindoll is my sister. For nearly half a century (!) this lady and I have been listening to each other, talking with each other, learning from each other, and especially laughing alongside each other. As a result, we know each other rather well and our love for each other is deep. In a relationship like ours, there aren't many stones left unturned or many feelings left unshared. It's beautiful.

While we may be close as brother and sister, our lifestyles are quite separate. As the pop song says, "two different worlds we live in." I am married and the father of four. She has never been married. My internal frame of reference is anchored to a domestic scene altogether different from hers. And even though "Aunt Luci" continues to be one of my family's all-time favorite people to spend time with, she is single (by choice) and therefore represents a slice of life not easily comprehended by most in a family-oriented society like ours. This is especially true if the single person is attractive, well-educated, happy, fulfilled, fun to be around, widely traveled, enjoying an authentic walk with God, and embraces a philosophy of life that is (even to some who are married) downright enviable.

Realizing how creative and gifted Luci is with a

pen in her hand, many months ago I began to urge
her to break the silence, to unveil the mystery, to open
the vault of her world so others could benefit by reading
her thoughts and tasting some of the fruit of her ever-
enlarging, enriching lifestyle. With so many wild and
weird ideas being offered to single persons these days—
much of it encouraging wrong attitudes and actions
without any biblical basis whatever—it seemed only
right to place into the hands of the public a book that
only Luci Swindoll could write. I am absolutely
delighted she took up the challenge! I am also proud
of her fine achievement.

I commend you for choosing *Wide My World,
Narrow My Bed*. Let me assure you ahead of time,
you're in for a treat. This isn't your plain vanilla,
predictable volume (thank goodness!), but a fresh,
carefully worded, honest presentation of singleness
from the viewpoint of one who knows what she is
writing about. It has weathered the test of time.

If you knew Luci as well as I, you would appreciate
her book all the more . . . for she is one of those rare
individuals whose life is as contagious as her style.

Charles R. Swindoll

Preface

When my mother died, eleven years ago this year, she was in the process of writing a book. It was to have been a volume about my younger brother, Chuck, including a compilation of his letters to the family from a certain period of his life that served greatly in forming his character: a tour of duty in the Marine Corps. They were marvelous letters which I have kept to this day—full of love, humor, faith, his interpretations of life, and the foundational strokes of God's Hand upon his early ministry and calling. But, due to mother's death, that book was never finished. Since then, however, Chuck has written ten books of his own, all published and highly successful. Additionally, my older brother, Orville, a missionary in Argentina for over twenty years, is an accomplished author, with his second book, in Spanish, having come off the press last year. My dad, too, left a legacy of letters that capture a romance for life and the tenderness and care of a father's heart.

So, the Swindolls are a rather wordy bunch, don't you agree? Consequently, when I was encouraged to write a book, who was I to say, "No"? I felt I had to carry on a tradition! In the course of my consideration, a friend asked me, "Luci, if you write a book, what *will you say?" "Say? . . . Mercy! I have no idea what I will <u>say</u>. I just feel it is something I have to <u>do</u>."*

But as I began to reflect back over my life, analyzing forty-nine years as a single person and recalling many of the events and crises that occurred during that time, I realized that perhaps there is something I have to say. Since one is often inclined to wax eloquent about the subjects he or she knows best, I would like to say some things about being single. My personal philosophy of the single life: how to live it and love it. Although I may not address anything that you've not heard before, I trust my suggestions will offer a fresh approach to what society calls "being alone." I'd like to show you how this condition can be happy, rich, fun, fulfilling . . . even preferred. Being single, or being alone, can provide the perfect opportunity for a very special relationship with the Lord that the two of you carve out together.

If you are not yet saturated with Swindoll diatribe from the printed page and are game to consider yet one more point of view, I give you this book, Dear Reader, as my statement and creed for life, liberty, and the pursuit of happiness. Thank you for picking up this book accidentally, because I know you are standing there now thinking, "Oh, I thought this was by one of her brothers. Hand Me Another Book!"

Luci Swindoll

Quotation

From birth to eighteen, a girl needs good parents.
From eighteen to thirty-five, she needs good looks.
From thirty-five to fifty-five, she needs a good
     personality.
From fifty-five on, she needs cash.[1]

—Sophie Tucker
Age 69

*I have always loved that quote. Even though it brings
a good laugh, there is a lot of truth in it. The only
phrase I might change is the last one—to include the
need for cash before age fifty-five. But who knows?
Maybe I'll need it more after.*

[1]Rosalind Russell and Chris Chase, *Life Is a
Banquet* (New York: Random House, 1977), p. 2.

Part One

GOOD PARENTS–
Looking Back

Chapter One – Childhood

Since my discovery of Dick Cavett some years ago, I have been one of his avid fans. I catch his interviews on television as often as I can. I've read his autobiography and I try to remember his one-liners to use at parties, claiming them as my own. In short, I think he is extremely witty and utterly charming. I often wish I had thought of the clever questions he asks in his interviews so I could incorporate them into my conversation.

Of particular interest to me was a precocious comment he made when he was not quite two, if you can imagine anyone verbalizing known thoughts at that age. His mother was carrying the young boy in her arms on a train when the conductor turned to her and asked, ". . . and how old is the baby?" to which the baby astonished everybody by booming out, "He will be two in November." When he told of this incident in his autobiography, his emphasis was upon the strangeness of anyone so young having such a deep voice. However, my fascination lay in the fact that a baby even knew his own age and was able to state it. It was a phenomenon of course. I have often since envisioned myself in such a situation: I, the baby, in my mother's arms, with someone saying

*to her, while looking at me, ". . . and I wonder what
your daughter wants to be when she grows up?" To
which I would respond, "Single!"*

*Of course, the idea of remaining unmarried did
not occur to me quite that young, but I honestly can't
ever remember a time when I wanted to marry. The
options for the unmarried person seemed to outweigh
the options for the married. But to remain single and
have that lifestyle as a goal in a home such as mine
when I was a child produced pressures and problems
that had to be dealt with frequently. My parents,
both Christians, taught us the truth of scripture from
our earliest years, and on many occasions we
memorized passages together. I remember from very
early in life one scripture that was frequently quoted
and certainly believed: Proverbs 22:6,* "Train up a
child in the way he should go: and when he is old, he
will not depart from it." *(King James Version . . . the
New American Standard wasn't out yet.) That's a
great verse, and one I heard often during my
childhood years. It was quoted by my grandparents
as a source of encouragement, quoted by my parents
to their three children as hope for the future, and
quoted by my brothers to me to remind me I was still
a child. And all the while I was of the opinion it didn't
even apply to me because I was "she," not "he."*

*Nevertheless, we were all taught to believe that
"in the way he should go" always included marriage.
Definitely no exceptions among practicing Christians,
and especially among Swindolls. One just got
trained, grew up, got married, and didn't depart.
That's how it was and that was simply doing the
right thing. However, as far back as I can remember
I had trouble believing in my own mind that marriage
had to be for everybody. Why did that teaching have
to be part of a child's training? And I was much older*

(and wiser!) before I realized for myself that it didn't. That particular verse has to do with the parents' sensitivity toward the child and their (the parents') personal investment of time in discovering the child's bents, or tendencies, and then guiding him or her in that direction. That is a whole different interpretation.

As I look back upon my childhood now, I know that in my parents' sincere efforts to rear their children in the truth of God's Word, they often did what they thought was right because of the dictates of their peers or society, not because they were knowledgeable of the bents in their children. My mother and father always pictured us in specific settings in the future, I'm sure: Their two sons would be successful businessmen who had used their various talents and abilities to rise to the top of some corporate ladder. Each had the brains to be a leader among leaders, and they would be making major decisions from enormous swivel chairs in oval offices, perhaps even the Oval Office. And their daughter (me!) would be the submissive, loving, self-sacrificing housewife and mother of four children, fulfilling the Christian calling for females. So I don't think they were totally prepared, initially, for my brothers' becoming ministers of the Gospel of Jesus Christ (as well as the fathers of four children each), although they always supported them with prayer and eventually were very proud of their callings.

I was the black sheep! Where was this submissive housewife/daughter they had envisioned? After all, it takes parents who are very secure within themselves to stand up to their Christian friends, look them boldly in the eye, and say, "No, our daughter isn't married because she prefers being single." Why, that was unheard of, especially in the *fifties. I mean <u>nobody</u> prefers that! It would have been easier for them to say, "She has two heads and no one wants to marry her," or "She has webbed fingers and can't wear the ring." You see, not getting married because you choose not to is hard to explain in our Christian culture.*

Isn't it a shame, single friends, that we don't have a scripture that reads:

> *Verily, verily, I say unto you, he that remaineth single will be of all people most blessed. His cares and worries will be minimal and he will never be broke.*

I would claim that promise every day. Talk about mercies that would be new every morning. Wow! But, alas, it is not so. There is no verse like that for the single person . . . but take heart, there isn't one for the married person either. Life isn't that uncomplicated for any human being.

Please understand, my parents were wonderful people. They were born again and were themselves products of Christian homes and training. I sincerely believe they wanted the very best for their children. My father was a faithful husband, a good provider, and a tender gentleman. He had a very cheerful outlook on life and a poetic soul. And he loved to laugh. My mother, on the other hand, was a creative fireball, full of energy and independence. She thought fast, talked fast, drove fast. In fact, a week before she died at age sixty-three, she got a traffic citation for speeding, and in all honesty told my father when she got home that she thought everybody else was driving too slowly. She sort of ripped through life, and in many ways was like a balloon on a string— always on the move. She was a very definite contrast to my father. They had two entirely different temperaments and dispositions, manifested in his stability and her vacillation of moods.

Because of this strong independent streak in my mother, she had her own way of thinking, and if one didn't blend in with her way there could be friction. Believe me, it was very difficult to say to her,

> Mother, I don't want to get married. I want to go to school and have a career. I want to sing professionally and travel and read books and have my own home and meet lots of people and dream my own dreams. How can I do all of that and be married too?

That would have been very hard for a person like my mother to understand.

Sound familiar? So often single people ask me,

> What can I do if my parents pressure me into getting married? I enjoy being single but they think I'm missing the boat if I don't settle down and have a family.

Somehow I find myself wanting to respond with, "Ask them to define 'settle down'," because it is certainly possible to be settled without a marriage partner and children. Whether there is marriage or singleness, one must be settled in one's philosophy of life in order to cope with the problems of life. I will be addressing this issue during the course of this book, because it is a very real frustration between parents and their unmarried offspring. It's sad, but true.

I did openly state to my mother my desire to remain single, and I greatly disappointed the domestic hopes she had for her only daughter. For a long period of time we operated under a cloud of disharmony that was not to be lifted completely until about ten years before she died. But it was during

those difficult years of separation in spirit from my
mother that I first began to know myself, and the
constant faithfulness of God became a comforting
reality. His grace did indeed prove sufficient. He took
those lonely years where there was fear and
uncertainty and began to acquaint me with many of
His unique and special ways of meeting needs. It
was my first time, really, to begin a personal
companionship with Him that was not an offshoot of
my parents' spiritual supervision. I wanted to know
Him for myself. I wanted His guidance and I needed
the courage and assurance that only He could
provide.

During this ten or eleven year period I discovered
many verses that seemed to be written just for me.
Here are three that I memorized during that time and
have recalled on countless occasions:

But He knows the way I take; When He has
tried me, I shall come forth as gold.   Job 23:10

And my God shall supply all your needs
according to His riches in glory in Christ
Jesus.   Philippians 4:19

Do not fear, for I am with you; Do not anxiously
look about you, for I am your God. I will
strengthen you, surely I will help you, Surely I
will uphold you with My righteous right
hand.   Isaiah 41:10

As a youngster I was told once by a Bible teacher
that God was always in the business of two things
regarding humanity. First, He was in the process of
bringing those who did not know Him to a knowledge
of Himself; and second, He was bringing those who
know Him to a place of maturity. The first process
would happen in a moment of time; the second would

take the rest of one's life.

I believe it was during this difficult decade in
my life that I began an in-depth relationship toward
maturity. God started showing me things about
myself that needed alteration (that class is still in
session, I might add), and I began to know Him as
the faithful Friend that He said He was. Additionally,
I must say that as I came to realize more about myself
and understood more of my reactions to life, I became
more aware of my need of Him. My relationship with
Him was very important to me. When Isaiah said,
". . . surely I will help you," he meant that for me,
too, in the twentieth century.

What I hadn't realized at the time was that I had
chosen a partner for my life. That choice, of course,
was the wisest I ever made.

Chapter Two - Credo

I have always been a goal-oriented person. I like to compete and take up "dares" when there is a jackpot at the end of the competition; it seems to make life more interesting. Even as a child I gravitated toward anything that had a reward in view. For instance, in the town where I grew up, the Saturday afternoon activity for my brothers and myself was to attend a local movie house, the Normana Theater, where we viewed a double feature, the RKO News, a weekly serial, and six or eight cartoons. On occasion there were contests conducted on stage, and more often than not I was one of the contestants.

I'll never forget the afternoon a prize was promised to the kid who ate the most Hershey bars in three minutes. Having this penchant for rewards, I volunteered, and by non-stop consumption managed to devour twelve Hersheys in the allotted time, setting an unprecedented record as the winner. Big deal! Somehow I envisioned the award as being a bicycle or watch or a year's supply of matinee tickets to the Normana. But I was mistaken. The judge handed me a box of twenty-four Hershey bars, and that was it. But I politely smiled with chocolate teeth and waddled offstage!

I love the feeling of accomplishing something, and being by nature a "finisher," I work best when there is a goal in my mind, whether that's at my office, in my home, or in my search for a full life. I have long-range goals that go past my retirement date and short-range goals that end today when the sun goes down. It's much like the wealthy lady who died and in her diary, found after her death, there was this scribbled note:

> Long-range goals:
>   1. Health—more leisure
>   2. Money
>   3. Write a book or a play—fame?
> Immediate goals:
>   1. Pick up pattern at Hilda's
>   2. Change faucets—call the plumber
>   (who?)
>   3. Try yogurt

I'm familiar with that immediate goal of "try yogurt." But for me, it's no longer on my list . . . it _is_ an accomplishment.

Goals seem to bring order out of confusion. They serve to guide us and make our thinking exact. There are times when life seems to blur or the outline of our desired accomplishment is hazy, making it impossible to fill in any blanks because the outline itself is not clear. "What do I want to do?" (How many times have you asked yourself that?) ". . . with this hour?" or ". . . in this circumstance?" or ". . . with my life?" While I am an advocate of goals for everyone, I would never advise someone to write down his or her every thought or hope or desire—that's not what I mean. To do that takes the spontaneity away from living and tends to box in all planning. I'm not talking about a rigid, structured model for daily living. That would lead us into a life of feeling trapped, as though the Spirit of God were unable to do His fresh, exciting work.

What I am referring to is what I call a "filter system" for life, or as I have also heard it termed, a "grid." Just as in the working of a machine—in a car or in an air-conditioner—there are filters or screens which serve to keep out that which is alien or unclean. If these machines had no filtering system, rejected nothing foreign that flew into them by mistake, or had no way of separating out what didn't belong there in order to keep them operating properly, very soon the machinery would stop. All that gunk would simply halt the process for which the machine was originally designed. Hence, the filter system serves as that very important grid for a smooth operation.

It is about that filter system for life that I want to address my thinking now. I personally feel that every adult needs his or her own grid through which decisions are made, causes are borne, and through which life is carried out. I feel it is important for men and women, old and young, married and unmarried. To me, it simplifies the confusion by which so much of life is characterized. Life doesn't become simple, but I think it does become easier. And . . . may I be dogmatic? I feel for the <u>successful</u> single it is mandatory. Define the basic needs of your life and work out a system for living that best meets those needs and that fits you and your personality. Get down to specifics as to who you are, what you want from life, and what your goals are in getting there.

We, as human beings, have needs on many levels—from basic physiological needs to those that are involved in our becoming our own persons, establishing our own autonomy. Needs are what effect behavior and motivate us toward a goal. In *other words, needs energize behavior; goals give direction to it. They force us to take action. It is virtually impossible to experience a need and not at least attempt to satisfy it in some way. I'm not saying all needs can be satisfied, but that is humanity's natural inclination. And if not satisfied, then pacified. At least the mollifying of a need causes its intensity to be appeased.*

However, the function of a need is not only to energize behavior; it is also to cause us to recognize deficiencies in our lives and makeup. This recognition guides us toward that object or end that we strive to obtain—our goals. Goals direct the energy that the need has produced. With this thought in mind, consider once again the idea of the grid we are trying to establish.

When I said earlier in this chapter that I feel it is mandatory for the successful single to have a filter system for his or her life, it is because it's too easy when one lives alone or operates alone, without a marriage partner, to feel sorry for one's self. There can be a lot of self-pity when nobody is there to share the load. I have wallowed in self-pity, so I know. I've not done it in a long time, but I have done it, and believe me—it leads nowhere. It is the proverbial dog chasing its tail. And . . . why stay there? We, the victims of that destructive thought process, are the only ones who can determine we're going to stop it and move ahead. And how much easier it is to move if we have a goal in mind. Goals provide purpose for our behavior and we don't have to go around in a circle. We can move ahead toward a standard we hope to achieve.

My personal filter system was written many years ago, after hours of reflection and soul searching, in order to determine what was important to me in life.

I call it <u>credo</u>. It is a guide by which I measure various phenomena to which I am exposed, and aids me greatly as a visual reminder of what I hold dear. For me, it is the highest example (in my own words) by which I filter data and measure long-range and immediate goals.

I would encourage you to write a credo for yourself—a realistic appraisal of what is important to you in terms of the foundation stones of your beliefs—and through the years re-read it to see if it still holds true. If you've been going in circles lately, as the dog chasing its tail, it will certainly help you get off that merry-go-round. Don't expect to sit down and dash it off in an hour or so. It takes time. Knowing ourselves takes time and aligning our beliefs with our personalities and tastes is a research project of the soul. But . . . don't let that stop you. Go for it! And use it as your tool for choices, causes, direction in crises, and in creative living. You'll love having that definition and it will serve you again and again. Mine has been a measurement for my life for over twenty years.

Credo

1. I believe in Jehovah God, the God of the Bible, to Whom I have access because of my trust in the justifying death of His Son, Jesus Christ.

2. I believe God to be an entity unto Himself, a Will without conflict, the Prime Mover of history, and the Personal Guide for my life by means of His Living Word (Jesus Christ) and His Written Word (the Bible).

3. I believe that no form or degree of reformation has ever been, can now be, or will ever be an adequate or satisfying substitute for God's plan for regeneration of the human heart, as stated in the

Bible.

4. I believe regeneration to be the absolutely essential factor for humanity to know the real meaning of life, and I believe this to be the first foundation stone to abundant living.

5. I believe Jesus Christ to be the unique Person of the universe: true and complete deity with perfect and sinless humanity united in one Person forever.

6. I believe all humanity to be born depraved and without hope until each person individually puts his or her trust in Jesus Christ (and Him alone) through an act of his or her own volition, as energized by God's Spirit.

7. I believe I will receive from life in direct proportion to that part of myself I am able and willing to give.

8. I believe individuals to be of more value than things, quality of more value than happiness, forgiveness of more value than pride, sincerity of more value than artificiality, and beauty of more value than adornment.

9. I believe in creative, industrious living that finds its source in a constructive challenge.

10. I believe in the expression of understanding and knowledge by means of reading, travel, the arts, observation, experience, and the best use of solitude.

11. I believe in the right of opinions and preferences, based upon consideration of known facts as well as Spirit-guided perception.

12. I believe in the power and motivation of positive thinking, a sense of humor, self-discipline, flexible planning, consideration and acceptance of others, open-mindedness, imagination, and self-control.

13. In summary, and on the basis of the above affirmation, I express this to be my true attitude and

I believe I should strive to be a demonstration of this confession on a consistent basis.

Chapter Three — Compromise

I recall some years ago, a dear friend of mine was contemplating matrimony. She was young, attractive, and well-educated, having graduated from college with honors, earning a degree in German. Her schooling had equipped her to hold a job with one of the major airlines, traveling all over the world. She had worked for them about eighteen months when a proposal for marriage came from the young man she had been dating. He was a ministerial student, on the brink of graduating from his Master's program in theology. A fine person. Kathy, my friend, was a sound Christian with high principles and a lot to offer a husband. But I remember her quandary over the idea of marriage and giving up the single life.

One day, in one of our many conversations about this state of uncertainty in her life, I said, "Kath', what is the primary reason for your hesitation in marrying Warren? I know you love him and I know you feel he is the person God has brought into your circumstances with whom you could share the rest of your life. What's the deal? Why don't you say 'yes'?" Li'l-Ole-Matchmaker-Me! I was ready to have her walk down that aisle because I felt that was what

*would make her happy. Marriage seemed to match
her temperament. (Please understand, too, that I
wasn't prying. Kathy and I were very good friends
and enjoyed a level of communication that was
characterized by this type of conversation.)*

*Her answer was, to me, an interesting one. She
said, "Well, Luci . . . if I say 'yes' to Warren, it is such
a big 'yes', affecting my life from now on. But if I say
'no', it is equally as big, and I realize that whatever I
say, I have given up one thing to have the other. By
saying 'yes' consciously I have automatically said
'no' to something else. It's such an important decision,
I want to weigh out not only the results of 'yes', but
the results of 'no' as well." I'll never forget that
response. I thought it not only said a lot about Kathy's
character, but it was a valid commentary on decision-
making that is rarely reduced to words.*

*Kathy had to make a very serious decision and
she wanted to do it with tremendous care because
the resulting consequences would accompany her for
the rest of her life. Incidentally, she did ultimately
say "yes" to Warren, and they were married. I sang
in their wedding and it was a beautiful, happy
occasion. She had made the right choice for herself,
based upon a conscious "yes" to one alternative as
well as "no" to the other. Kathy had entered the real
world of concession and she had done it thoughtfully,
with both feet on the ground. She had carefully
chosen a style of living that reflected her
temperament—marriage.*

*When we enter the adult world, leaving our
childhood behind us with its innocence and naiveté,
we soon find that the art of living life—any lifestyle
of our choosing—is a full-time occupation and
responsibility. There are values to be established,
obligations to be met, decisions to be made, crosses*

*to be borne. We begin to see for ourselves that few
situations in life are ideal. There are numerous
adjustments we must make daily in our thinking in
order to cope with what is real, and there is no
escaping reality with its need for concessions. Outside
the restrictions of our parents' instruction, we must
choose for ourselves what paths we want to follow,
with the understanding that each time we say "yes"
to one thing, we automatically say "no" to something
else, often without conscious thought. We learn that
we simply cannot have everything we want in life.*

*In choosing what we do want, however, we must
give up one thing to have something else; we must
be constantly adjusting to opposing demands or
issues. To live in a real world we will always need
to surrender (at least partially) some position of
thought or action in order to embrace another. We
need to compromise.*

*Because life is basically a serious matter, our
most important decisions are of a serious nature. If
we opt to live life apart from a personal relationship
with God, that is a grave decision with eternal
consequences. But it is no more critical or serious a
decision than choosing Christ and walking with God.
It, too, has eternal consequences. Each calls for
certain requirements regarding our standard of living.
If we decide to marry and live with a partner, life
takes on subsequent responsibilities to make that
arrangement work. We need to think out these
responsibilities carefully . . . we must come to grips
not only with what we hope to gain in marriage, but
with what we think we will forfeit by not remaining
single, as well.*

*In an effort to choose any lifestyle correctly and
in harmony with one's temperament, personality,
and bents (especially as it relates to being single),*

will you consider, with me, a few thoughts.

The happiest single people I know are those who are involved with life, not standing on the sidelines, enduring their plight, waiting for something better to come along. In fact, the happiest people I know, in general, are those actively engaged in living, entering into the rhythm of life.

Why is it that so many single people feel that marriage is <u>the</u> answer? Married people can be very unhappy, unfulfilled people, too. A former boss of mine—a single man whom I love dearly—and I, used to talk about going into the counseling profession together. We would place our names, as counselors, on the same shingle outside our office, because people with whom we worked were always asking our advice on problems. And the majority of our "clientele" were marrieds . . . asking for recommendations for ways to cope with marriage problems! Here we were, happy singles, giving advice to the unhappy marrieds. It was a crazy role to be in, certainly, but it revealed to us that many people who marry simply say "yes" to that lifestyle without conscious consideration of what their automatic "no" to remaining single means. They never think about the compromises that must be made to live either life. And . . . they never look at their temperaments in light of making decisions about the major issues of life.

At this point, I would like to suggest two important areas you might ponder, in your own life, that will help you determine whether or not you have a temperament which is conducive to living (and enjoying!) the single life. Keep in mind the fact that you can make mental concessions along the way as you think this through. As you examine your thoughts and see that you are more strongly bent toward one

trait than another, that does not mean you are devoid
of its opposite. For instance, just because you are
basically an independent person does not mean you
have no areas of dependency. Perhaps you are more
independent than dependent, but don't be absolute.
Our makeups give us room for both strengths and
weaknesses.

First of all, what we are looking for in our
temperament pictures are the broad strokes of life
which enable us to recognize patterns in our behavior.
Patterns are established, initially, on an unconscious
level; then, as they repeat themselves again and
again in the course of our lives, we can bring them to
a level of consciousness. I say "can" because it is
possible to go blithely through life in such a benign
manner that the awareness, much less recognition,
of patterns would never enter one's stream of
consciousness. For some individuals there is such a
lack of concern for value in any realm that they seem
to "skip" through life. They wouldn't recognize a
behavior pattern if it hit them in the face!

Patterns enable us to monitor our profiles. In their
predictable repetition they help us chart our
temperaments and they are the foundation blocks of
our living—our lifestyle! Here are some of the
questions you might ask yourself in your effort to
determine whether or not you are cut out for the single
lifestyle. Look for the answer in your behavior
patterns.

1. When I am alone, can I be content?
2. Am I a self-starter?
3. When things go wrong, can I laugh at my
   dilemma or do I need someone else to pull
   me up?
4. Is the majority of my time spent in

constructive growth or stagnation?
5. How much do I lean on other people?
6. In crisis situations, do I usually panic?

These are, of course, a cross-section of questions that can apply to anyone. I use them as an example of a means of monitoring one's behavior in an effort to determine patterns, not necessarily to encourage the making of a choice prior to the recognition of a need. Be assured that I do not advocate a decision regarding marriage or remaining single prior to God's timing. I am not one who feels such a choice has to be made at the expense of knowing one's own bents or temperament. Choosing marriage or single life should be predicated upon the knowledge of one's temperament, I feel; therefore, these aren't the only questions by far. Make up your own, then ask them of yourself.

Second, the real secret of discovering one's temperament is knowing one's self. This means not only knowing that part of us that we know well and can predict always, but that part of us that slumbers within our core—the self we do not know well and have trouble predicting. One helpful way to search out this knowledge is to ask "why" in various situations.

1. Why did I behave in that manner?
2. Why did I laugh at that when it was at someone else's expense?
3. Why don't I find joy in what I'm doing?
4. Why am I lonely?
5. Why have I lost my homeostasis?

As we attempt to answer these questions, honestly answer them within our heart of hearts, we come to know our temperaments. Couple this knowledge with an awareness of the predictability of patterns, and I think we should be able to choose a lifestyle which is compatible with our particular temperament.

Does all this seem hard? It is hard—a full-time occupation and responsibility, as I said earlier in this chapter. But the joys of knowing will definitely outweigh the difficulties of self-examination.

With this knowledge and awareness under our belts now, and with the realization that life can be a choice to enjoy rather than a plight to endure, let's talk about the balance that lies between what is ideal and what is real. This is the plane on which we will live out our lives most comfortably, whichever lifestyle we choose. Extremes are what kill us! They kill our enthusiasm; they kill our hopes; they kill our energies, our drives, our passions. We must achieve a balance if we desire to rise above a prosaic existence characterized by futility and apathy. Neither can we live, however, in the realm of lofty aspirations and perfection, marked by idealistic pursuits. If we attempt to do that our expectations will be dashed at every turn.

Therefore, in the remainder of this chapter, I want to discuss the issue that builds a balanced life for all of us—something we have already touched upon, the issue of compromise. By saying that, I know many of you will look at the word "compromise" and will think I am recommending the dissolution of one's principles. That's not true. If you re-read my Credo, you'll see how far from the truth that is. By compromise I mean mentally negotiating toward a settlement in one's own mind between the two worlds of the ideal and the real . . . finding a way to live life on a balanced plane.

If we do not find the balance needed for healthy living, we will tend to experience life in one of two *extremes. We may exist in a dream world of idealism much as Cervantes' seventeenth century protagonist, Don Quixote. As a romantic idealist unable to live with reality, he went about life attempting to redress the wrongs of the whole world. He ultimately returned home to La Mancha shortly before he died, frustrated and mocked. Or . . . we will live such a practical, ordinary, materialistic, boring life that all the poetry of our souls will be negated, if not destroyed. (Dare I even mention legalism as an extreme? It is the worst blight that ever fell upon the good news of the Gospel, withering hope and growth in Christ because of its demands for performance. It nullifies the authentic sweet work of God's Spirit and is as dangerous a way to live as being too idealistic or too realistic. May God help the person . . . and those around him . . . who chooses that lifestyle.) Any of these extremes lead to disappointment time and time again.*

Personally, my natural tendency is toward idealism. I am a romantic and must constantly fight a quixotic nature. Somehow, in any given situation, my first thought is, "Utopia is over that hill." And when it is not there, I tend to think I have simply climbed the wrong hill. I want to believe the best of people and find myself making up something good if it's not readily apparent. Even as an adult I have trouble believing someone would actually "do me in." As I said, a true idealist! It is hard for me to believe that situations do not live up to my expectations, my dreams. And, as a result I am often disappointed. I'm certainly not the gullible, impractical person I once was, but if I ever lean toward an extreme, it would surely be toward idealism. Often, the dream in my mind is, to me, the reality. Let me give you an example.

When I moved to California from Texas, eight

*years ago, I was going to take the world by the tail.
Excitement was in the air! I had lived in Texas all
my life and now I was going to live in an entirely
new environment. I took a long time saying good-bye
to my friends there—lots of parties, farewell festivities,
and genuine tears that accompany departures. But
. . . I was thrilled with the dream of a new adventure
for my life. Everyone assured me that I was going to
love my new job and new opportunities. I was
unafraid, self-confident, and headed for success! My
brother, Chuck, flew to Dallas to drive with me to
California and we were both excited about the
prognosis for the future. I dreamed of discovering
Hollywood and of Hollywood discovering me. TEXAS
GIRL MAKES GOOD: I could envision the headlines
back home!*

*We arrived after a delightful, laugh-filled, three-
day trip of brother/sister camaraderie, and I moved
into a beautiful, clean apartment with many luxuries
available for the tenants. I could see an enormous
mountain out my back window to the north, and the
sea was only forty-five minutes from my apartment,
to the south. Yes! So far, my dream was coming true.*

*But . . . after a week of getting things unpacked,
making my apartment into a home, visiting with
family and new friends, I went to work for the first
time and reality began to stare me in the face. My
job was not at all what I had envisioned. In Dallas,
where I worked in Research for eighteen years, the
emphasis was on academia. There was a lot of
freedom, an air of creativity, visiting with fellow
workers and friends—hard work in a fun atmosphere.
Certain friends of mine even referred to it as "The
Country Club" because it was such a pleasant place
of employment.*

The job in California, on the other hand, was

entirely different. It was in Pipeline work and the emphasis was on production. The work itself was difficult and totally unknown to me. There was a lot of math and I wasn't good at math. Idle chatter was discouraged and I was accustomed to spontaneous verbal interaction. Deadlines were strict in production where they were more lax in academia. In short, the work, the office, the personnel were not living up to my dream. Then . . . there was the freeway! Or, the Chariot Race, as I call it. I had long drives to and from a job I tolerated, but in which I had no zest. Even my new friends and my family with their support and encouragement could not lift the trauma from my soul. They did everything humanly possible, but it was a war that I had to fight and win myself in order to be at peace.

The battle between my dreams and reality went on for weeks, months, really for two years. I cried out to God more than once, "What happened? Where is everything I wanted? Why is all this so hard? Why am I not happy? Please help me!" I confess to you that it was a dark period in my life. I agonized over my state. My idealistic dream had met with my realistic life. In order to cope with life as it was, I was going to have to compromise between what was ideal and what was real. And, in time, God taught me the lesson I am sharing with you now.

The life I had envisioned for myself in California never existed—it was a figment of my romantic imagination. In my new job, new surroundings, new friends, new environment situation, I eventually had to realize that everything was not perfect and was never going to be perfect. But . . . neither was everything as terrible as I thought it was. I finally found a happy medium—a compromise—and I learned to live there. And, it worked!

Ironically enough, I am now no longer in that job. It appears as though once God got that seed of information lodged into my thick skull, He gave me a promotion. And of course, I am grateful. But that particularly difficult period was a tremendous learning experience. In many ways, it was an area in which I matured for the first time.

Are you having a similar experience? If so, I would challenge you to search out a balance for your dilemma. It does exist, I assure you. Ask God to guide you in that search. He will do it, and the by-product of His deliverance could very well be the learning of an important lesson He is wanting to teach you. That will be a more valued commodity than a change in your circumstances. Lessons learned always are.

When I have ceased to break my wings
Against the faultiness of things,
And learned that compromises wait
Behind each hardly opened gate,
When I can look Life in the eyes,
Grown calm and very coldly wise,
Life will have given me the Truth,
And taken in exchange—my youth.[1]

Sara Teasdale
Age 33

[1]Reprinted with permission of Macmillan Publishing Co., Inc. from *Collected Poems* by Sara Teasdale. Copyright 1917 by Macmillan Publishing Co., Inc., renewed 1945 by Mamie T. Wheless.

Part Two

GOOD LOOKS–
Looking Out

Chapter Four – Health

There is an excessive amount of information written on the subject of health, and when I consider adding one more comment to that topic, I lose mine. I get a headache. Not long ago I was in a local bookstore, investigating one of the many new books on dieting, and discovered there was an entire Diet Section in the store. It was full of overweight people, lethargically pulling the volumes from the shelves and leafing through pages of information pertaining to newer and better ways to take off inches and pounds. A few were talking about that four-letter word which seems to dominate the English language— DIET.

And that isn't all. In the aisle next to the one where we were solving the problems of the avoirdupois, there were three ladies poring over a new book on exercise . . . running, I believe it was. They looked fabulous. Tan. Thin. Sleek. Perfect. Yet, they confessed to one another their desire to run at least one more mile next time . . . to get an even richer tan . . . to work out at the Club more faithfully. All of our team in the Diet Section were trying not to listen as they rehearsed their goals, since they, no doubt, were already outdistancing us in every way. I simply *resumed munching my Almond Joy.*

After locating the book I was seeking, I picked it up and started toward the cash register. On my way, I walked through an aisle labeled MENTAL HEALTH. These publications ranged from books on transcendental meditation to a volume entitled <u>Mental Gymnastics—Exercising While You Wait</u>. *The person holding a copy of that appeared as though he were. His eyes were closed and I was certain he was either in a trance or not among the living, when suddenly, his eyes popped open and he realized I was looking straight at him. "Oh, I'm not doing a gymnastic," he said. "My contacts are killing me and I was trying to rest my eyes." We exchanged a few lines about the price we all pay for vanity, then we parted, the same strangers we were when we met.*

On my way back to work I started thinking about all the books that must have been written on health. Countless thousands. And not only books! Good health is touted on television, radio, and in films. National magazines are replete with recommended ways to be healthy and stay healthy. Of course, we all know why. Health is a treasure and fitness is an enviable state for anyone. When we have healthy minds, bodies, and spirits, we have personal assurance that we will be strong enough and sound enough to live our lives fully, coping effectively with life's problems rather than being the victim of them. And who doesn't envy that? Everybody wants to feel good. It's the natural desire of human nature. On the other hand, when we are burdened with a problem in our minds or bodies, little else seems to go well. We cannot ignore it and expect it to go away. Humanly speaking, being well is almost synonymous with being happy. It's hard to be happy and in pain at the same time.

Because there is so much specific information available on the subject of health, I will not go into detail about the treatment of various ailments. That is not my purpose, and certainly I am not qualified to speak to that issue. Rather, in the space available here, I would like to present some ideas that seem to be suitable and practical in forming an awareness toward a healthy body, mind, and spirit.

For the most part, I have the single person in view as I write, but these comments can apply, generally, to married folks as well. These ideas are what I call "Maintenance Principles," in that they spring from a standpoint of preventive remedies. Some of them are quite simple to apply. Others are more complex, requiring the element of trust and faith, as it regards the unknown factors of our physical bodies and emotional and spiritual psyches.

Before I launch into these principles, let me make one general statement about good health. Since we are made up of flesh and blood as well as minds and spirits, there are certain things we should do to have good health, as well as certain ways we should be. Ideally, of course, it would be great to always face life with hope, optimism, purpose, and trust, as we move about in a body that is free of stress, pain, or fear.

But few things in life are ideal, as we saw in Chapter 3. Realistically, therefore, we must admit that the living of daily life produces all sorts of inner factions and tensions that can manifest themselves in physical pain, mental anguish, and spiritual depression. Surely, no one has trouble admitting that! That's the way things are. But . . . as we grasp good principles for healthy living, as we learn that we can prevent certain ills from occurring by simply using our heads, and as we realize that God provides *marvelous promises for His children to claim and rely on when we are not well, the prognosis for a sound and healthy life becomes brighter and more probable.*

As I said earlier, however, to achieve this kind of thinking and to live on this plane, one must DO certain things to provide physical well-being, and BE certain ways to maintain the homeostasis required for one's psyche. I have hanging on the wall of my office a clever saying that reminds me of this need for balance between doing and being:

TO DO IS TO BE

—Plato

TO BE IS TO DO

—Sartre

TO DO BE DO BE DO

—Sinatra

I think "ol' Blue Eyes" has the best outlook of all, don't you?

Maintenance Principles

For the sake of order and form I have broken down the subject of health into three categories: the <u>body</u>, the <u>mind</u>, and the <u>spirit</u>. Then, under each of these headings I've listed five principles that can be applied to these categories, as well as scripture passages that I hope will be beneficial in dealing with this issue of maintaining good health in your own life. Some of these principles may seem a bit weather-beaten with use; nevertheless, they are the ones which surface again and again in my life as being the best remedies for the perpetuation of health. Remember—so much of life is what we make it. And we can make it even better when we are well.

The Body

DO your body a favor—think nutrition.
BE alert—the sleep you lose will be your own.
DO what your doctor advises—get that checkup.
BE sure your teeth are clean—then smile.
DO your favorite exercise—but do it regularly.

I urge you therefore, brethren, by the mercies of God, to present your bodies a living and holy sacrifice, acceptable to God, which is your spiritual service of worship.

Romans 12:1

My son, give attention to my words; Incline your ear to my sayings. Do not let them depart from your sight; Keep them in the midst of your heart. For they are life to those who find them, And health to all their whole body.

Proverbs 4:20-22

Flee immorality. Every other sin that a man commits is outside the body, but the immoral man sins against his own body. Or do you not know that your body is a temple of the Holy Spirit who is in you, whom you have from God, and that you are not your own? For you have been bought with a price: therefore glorify God in your body.

1 Corinthians 6:18-20

The Mind

DO things in the order of their importance—one
*   at a time.*
BE flexible—life is full of change.
DO battle with the thing that holds you down—
*   regret, bitterness, guilt, fear.*
BE patient with yourself—character isn't built in
*   a day.*

DO a mental gymnastic that has lasting value—
memorize scripture.

And do not be conformed to this world,
but be transformed by the renewing of your
mind, that you may prove what the will of
God is, that which is good and acceptable and
perfect.   Romans 12:2

For God has not given us a spirit of
timidity, but of power and love and discipline.
2 Timothy 1:7

Thou wilt keep him in perfect peace, whose
mind is stayed on thee: because he trusteth
in thee. Trust ye in the LORD for ever: for in
the LORD JEHOVAH is everlasting strength.
Isaiah 26:3, 4 (KJV)

The Spirit

DO something constructive with your solitude—
spend time in praise.
BE involved in activities that feed your soul—not
your appetites.
DO a number on the devil—trust in the Lord.
BE aware of correct priorities—both spiritual and
emotional.
DO one of God's hardest commandments—
forgive.

Why are you in despair, O my soul? And
why have you become disturbed within me?
Hope in God, for I shall yet praise Him, The
help of my countenance, and my God.
Psalm 42:11

He who is slow to anger is better than the
mighty, And he who rules his spirit, than he
who captures a city.   Proverbs 16:32

And let not your adornment be merely
external . . . but let it be the hidden person of
the heart, with the imperishable quality of a
gentle and quiet spirit, which is precious in
the sight of God.   1 Peter 3:3, 4

*Health for the whole person: the body, the mind, the
spirit. That should be our goal. And this will be my
prayer:*

Beloved, I pray that in all respects you
may prosper and be in good health, just as
your soul prospers.   3 John 2

*In conclusion, I would like to add this: One of
the most desirable traits a person can possess, in
terms of maintaining good health, is a sense of humor.
We have all heard the phrase, "Laughter is the best
medicine," and I could not agree more. Do you wonder
why, then, I've not mentioned it thus far in this
chapter? I'll tell you. A sense of humor and being
able to laugh at life and at one's self is, to me, a
characteristic of top priority in a person's makeup.
This chapter could never hold all I have to say on
the subject. It gets a chapter of its own. Turn the
page!*

It was a cold, dreary Sunday afternoon in
November . . . about that time of day when you realize
you've spent most of your energy on the weekend,
there's only a matter of hours left until Monday
morning when the tasks of a new work week become
an actuality, and you've simply got the blahs. You
know the situation. I call it the "SES"—Sunday
Evening Syndrome.

Anyway, due to the weather, the SES, and the
fact that I was still somewhat new in California and
had not yet made many friends, I was blue and
borderline lonely. I related this condition to my jocular
friend, Marilyn Meberg, about whom you will read
later in the book. She, being the nonpareil listener
that she is, gave close attention to both my words
and my spirit in an effort to help lift me from this
period of loneliness. The conversation went
something like this:

Luci: I can't seem to get out of the doldrums,
    Marilyn, yet I love California and I
    feel this is where the Lord wants me
    to be . . . but I wish I had some single
    friends to do things with. You don't

> know what loneliness is! You're
> married and you can't fully under-
> stand loneliness unless you're
> single.
>
> Marilyn: Luci, don't think that only single
> people feel lonely; anybody can be
> lonely. Marriage doesn't preclude
> loneliness.
>
> (I was quiet for a moment, trying to
> remember what "preclude" meant.)
>
> Luci: What does "preclude" mean? I can't
> remember.
>
> Marilyn: I don't know. But Rachmaninoff wrote
> one!

Immediately I broke into laughter. What a marvelous line and how it lifted my spirit! Even now, years later, as I reflect upon that conversation and, most especially, upon Marilyn's creative witticism, I laugh. It was so totally unexpected and so utterly non sequitur, falling like a verbal guillotine upon my train of thought, that not only did I find it funny, but it served as the catalyst to change my mood.

Humor, in its many-splendored varieties, is a remarkable thing. Henri Bergson, the French philosopher, said, "Humor is a momentary anesthesia of the heart," and truly it is. A good laugh can aid in deadening the pain and difficulty that is frequently a part of our daily living. It can cross the barrier of language or culture. It can erase tension in a business meeting or a misunderstanding between friends. It can liven up a discussion or a school room, an office or a family. And it can certainly relieve boredom. We all love to be around people who seem to have nonsense in their veins, and, even more preferably, we desire to have it in our own psychological makeup.

Interestingly enough, laughter really serves no biological purpose. It is essentially a reflex action, sometimes called a "luxury reflex" because it is quite unrelated to humanity's struggle for survival. Yet the emotional service it provides as a release from repressed tension cannot be measured. To analyze humor, wit, or laughter is a task as delicate and difficult as analyzing the composition of a perfume with its multiple ingredients. It defies analysis.

Have you ever come home from work or school and thought, "Gee, I'd love to have a good laugh. But nobody's here and nothing is funny"? So you switch on the TV, hoping to find the laughter you want, thinking, "Entertain me . . . make me laugh!" I find no fault with that, really, unless it serves as a crutch and is our primary source of entertainment. But I believe people can be more creative than that—with just a little imagination.

Last summer, for instance, when I arrived home from my office one evening, I had that urge to laugh but nothing seemed funny. I checked the mail, only to find one item in my box—and it was a postcard delivered to my house by mistake. The number was the same as mine but the street was different. I love to receive mail, so I thought, "Shoot, one piece of mail and it's not even for me. Oh well, I guess I'll read it anyway. Maybe it'll have something in it that will give me a chuckle." Wrong! Friends, that postcard was the most inane communiqué I have ever seen. It read:

Dear Jane,

The drive here was nice. We stopped for a bite to eat at a nice place on the way. The coffee was cold but the food was pretty good.

Stanley said their gravy tasted as good as mine. But I think mine's better. We sure are having a nice time. See you soon.

Bye-bye and love,
Dorothy

"Good grief," I thought. "That's one of the worst pieces of mail I have ever read in my life. It says <u>nothing</u>. Whoever Jane is, she's going to be disappointed, poor soul—I think I'll add a line." So . . . I practiced scribbling out my thoughts on a piece of scratch paper to achieve the same style of writing, using the same size pen point and color. Then I added: "P.S. Jerry's leg is so much better. Practically healed."

Now don't you think that helped? It gave the reader something to ponder, and as I dropped it in the mail, it gave me the laugh I was looking for.

Was that cruel to do? Do you think it caused someone to worry unnecessarily? I have heard that the coarsest type of humor is the practical joke, but I think not, unless there is malicious intent. I meant no offense of any kind and that practical joke carried no malice. I was making something amusing (to me anyway) out of a moment of disappointment. And again, upon reflection (like the "preclude" story), it still produces a light spirit in me. It was a crazy gag, done out of fun.

Do you ever do that for yourself? If not, you should! I'm not suggesting that you crawl into the corner postal box and edit all dull correspondence. I'm suggesting, "When life gives you a lemon, make lemonade." In the disappointments of life, set about to create what humor you can. It is amazing what you will come up with, and the fun you can have—all by yourself. Just as important, too, when you think

back on those times, you'll enjoy the moment afresh.
It's a great way to win over predicaments.

As a case in point, let me tell you about a nutty
contest I had with myself earlier this year—born out
of a predicament. In April I was asked to be the soloist
at my nephew's wedding. It was to be a large church
wedding, officiated by the two fathers—father of the
bride and father of the groom—both ministers. Months
of planning had gone into this big event. I was
advised of the colors that had been chosen, and it
was suggested I wear a formal in keeping with the
color scheme.

My first inclination was to buy a new dress for
the occasion. But as I reconsidered my finances
carefully and realized such an expenditure would
be unwise in light of other obligations during the
month, I decided to wear a formal I already had.
Admittedly, it had been around awhile and needed
a bit of alteration and repair, but it was exactly the
right colors and would serve my purpose well. After
all, I was only the soloist . . . not the bride!

Under the inspiration of that inventive idea, I
took the dress to the cleaners (I am not a seamstress,
unfortunately) to ask their advice on letting out the
hem, patching up a small hole at the neckline, having
it cleaned and pressed, etc. No problem! They assured
me they would be able to do all I requested and in
plenty of time before the wedding. The fabric was
somewhat old; nevertheless, it would accommodate
this event and be fine. I left the cleaners, very pleased
with my idea—in a jubilant spirit about the whole
thing.

On the morning of the wedding I picked up the
dress and it did indeed look terrific. I brought it home
and about two hours before I was due at the church,
I decided to try it on. Proper length, cleaned, pressed,

and with flowers at my neck, even the patched hole
would be covered. "Smart girl," I was thinking as I
sat down to put on the pair of heels I had planned to
wear with it. Then I stood up. Just as I did, my right
heel caught in the hem, and upon standing I heard
RRRRRRIIIP! Without looking, I sat down . . . and my
thoughts were, "Oh no. This <u>can</u> <u>not</u> be." I couldn't
look. I lowered my head and sat quietly for a moment.
Then I said, out loud:

> Lord, You know how I've planned on
> wearing this dress to the wedding—but did
> You hear that rip? I have probably torn the
> back out of this old thing. Now what? What
> am I going to do? I have two hours for this
> dress to be healed or whatever . . .

I just sat there, afraid to look at the damage,
when suddenly it struck me, "Luci . . . this isn't the
end of the world. Life's going to go on whether you go
to that wedding or not, or whether you sing or not.
Now shape up, kid. Make lemonade! You can think
of something creative. Use your imagination." And I
began to laugh. I don't know why, except the
incongruity of this turn of events in light of my brilliant
preparations struck me funny. And mind you, at this
point I hadn't even looked at the dress or stood up.
All I could do was laugh.

Finally I got up. As expected, there was the
evidence of heel in hem—a large, irregular tear of
the fabric just above the hemline. I could hardly
believe it, but it was definitely a predicament with a
very real opportunity to be creative. First, I got out of
the dress and dashed back to the cleaners faster than
a speeding bullet to see if they could repair that spot
hurriedly. They could and did. Second, I decided,
"I'll wear this old rag to the wedding as its swan song

before it retires from active service. And for every person who says anything positive about the dress, I'll take five dollars out of my savings toward the purchase of a new dress." Then I made two rules for my contest:

1. *The comment had to include the word "dress", not just a general remark about my looks or grooming. It had to be specific.*

2. *I could not tell anyone about this until after it was over. It was a private affair between the disappointed side of me and the creative side.*

As I dressed for the ceremony, I found I could hardly wait—not only for the nuptials, but for the reception as well, where the majority of my contest would occur as people visited together. No longer was I thinking, "I'll make do with what I've got." I was anticipating a very enjoyable and legitimate justification for the eventual purchase of a new dress. The predicament became a springboard for a lot of fun. So off I went!

During the course of the evening, I received six direct compliments about that formal. Can you believe it? One dear old man said, "Luci, you look so pretty. Is that a new dress?" Of course, he is blind, but I got the five dollars just the same. I loved the whole occasion, and my creative side made thirty bucks.

As I was getting ready for bed that night, I was glad I had reacted to that problem as I had. I don't always do that, even though it is my general nature to respond to disappointments or unpleasant situations creatively. Of course, I could have gone out and bought a new dress afterwards, contest or no contest. But this method of proposed purchase gave my evening verve and enthusiasm, which was what my spirit needed for that moment . . . and that's what a sense of humor is all about.

How do you react in similar circumstances? Ask yourself. Do you look for a way to find happiness or zest by transforming what could be self-pity or bitterness into fun and laughter? Or do you just give in . . . give up, and join the ranks of "if-anything-bad-can-happen-it-will-happen-to-me" people? Granted, every dilemma does not have a humorous side, but I believe more do than we realize, if we simply look for them.

Let me give you an account of one of the most illogical moments of humor that has ever occurred in my life. From start to finish it was bizarre, funny, and as ludicrous to explain as this old Yiddish proverb I once heard: "If the rich could hire other people to die for them, the poor could make a wonderful living."

Last September 8 was my birthday. I turned forty-nine, the big year before my half-century mark. I have never objected to telling my age—all my friends know that—and I've always made a celebration out of birthdays, both my own and my associates'! Anyone who knows me well recognizes this as one of my patterns. Therefore, I thought nothing strange or unusual when three of my "pals," Marlene, Carla, and Sharon, requested that I keep a Saturday afternoon and evening free (around September 8) to celebrate this event. All they said was, "We'll pick you up at your house at 12:00 noon. Dress comfortably—shorts or jeans—and bring other clothes (something nice) to change into for dinner." These instructions were given to me five weeks before the

celebration was to take place, one afternoon when
we went roller skating (another mad moment in
history!).

"OK!" I agreed and began to look forward to the
culmination of their high-powered, secretive
planning. On September 12 I looked out my front
window at noon and there in front of my house
appeared Marlene, Carla, Sharon . . . and a 1960
hearse. That's right: a long, silver job with a black
vinyl top and blue curtains. To put it mildly, I stared!
I expected one of their "real" cars to pull up behind
them. But it didn't come. Marlene bounded up to my
door, announced that they had arrived to pick me
up, and were all set to "do the town." In the midst of
my laughter and incredulity, I ambled out to this
vehicle. Sharon, wearing a black derby, leaped out
from behind the steering wheel and opened the door
for me . . . or I should say "side"—on a hearse, the
entire side opens. They had covered the area behind
the driver's seat with quilts, pillows, beach towels,
and a sheet in order to make it as comfortable as
possible, since this was to be our home-away-from-
home for the remainder of the afternoon and evening.
We got in, laughing, talking, and taking pictures, as
Sharon resumed her position as chauffeur and official
guide for our upcoming escapade.

Naturally, all my neighbors wondered who died
as we pulled away from my street into the waiting
world. However, as music and shrieks of laughter
emanated from inside "Patty" (our name for the
vehicle—after "Patty Hearse"), the looks of sadness
on people's faces changed to astonishment. "What is
it?" was more the look, as opposed to "Who died?"

And, Dear Readers . . . we did indeed "do the
town." We careened onto and off of the Los Angeles
freeways . . . we went to the L.A. Arboretum and

Huntington Library . . . we stopped at a grocery store . . . we changed clothes in a public restroom . . . we attended the Los Angeles Ballet . . . we even ate dinner at "Tommy's"—a drive-in hamburger joint (dressed to the teeth, of course). My hostesses ordered hamburgers, cokes, and french fries for four and served them on a card table covered with lace cloth and silver candle holders, which they had brought from home and had set up with chairs next to Patty Hearse! And in all of it, we never stopped laughing or snapping pictures or waving to people or explaining that we were <u>not</u> a group of hippies living in the back of an old hearse. But little did we know . . . the best was yet to come.

About 10:30 P.M., after the ballet, the final stop on their planned agenda was to have coffee and dessert at the Bonaventure Hotel in downtown Los Angeles. Sharon found an ideal parking place immediately across the street from the front door of the hotel. We got out, crossed the street, looked back at "Patty", and remarked among ourselves that this had indeed been a birthday to remember. What fun! What photographs and memories we'll have! What will we do when I'm fifty, to top this? (My friends told me that the place that rented the hearse to them also rents Sherman tanks. Maybe I can move away before I'm fifty!)

After coffee and a walk around the hotel, we all decided to call a halt to these crazy shenanigans and head for home. It was five minutes to midnight. So we walked outside, hurried toward "Patty" . . . and IT WAS GONE. I said, "OK gang, where is it? What's the next trick?" They were stunned. They stared at the vacant parking place, looked at each other, then at me, and said, "Luci, we're not kidding; the hearse has been stolen." I was, at this point, in stitches—beside myself with laughter. Marlene, too. We doubled over in hysteria, absolutely no help with the problem at hand. Eventually, when we realized that Carla and Sharon were sincerely distraught over the disappearance of the vehicle which they had rented and for which they were responsible, we managed to straighten up somewhat. Now what had been a joyful, carefree day became a serious predicament.

We went back into the hotel, called the police (which was hilarious in itself—trying to explain that our rented hearse had been stolen), only to find out it had been towed to the car pound because we had parked illegally. For forty-two dollars we could get the vehicle that night. We checked our purses, pooled our resources, and came up with exactly the amount we needed.

Later, as we were waiting in the pound to free "Patty", lined up on an old wooden bench, staring out a window onto the darkened streets of LA, I said, "Girls, savor this moment. This won't ever happen again in your lives. Someday you'll tell your kids about this night and you'll revel again in its memory. The best part of the whole day is this—sitting here in a car pound. So crazy. So unexpected. This is great."

On the way home that night—tired, happy, content, and mellow, I thought again of the tremendous value of a sense of humor and the important part it plays in our daily living. It can see us through many of life's tight spots, and release the tension of a pressure situation. It can give us a laugh upon reflection when we are alone. It can even preclude loneliness.

Ask Rachmaninoff. He wrote one.

Chapter Six
Hospitality

Life passes like a flash of lightning
Whose blaze barely lasts long enough to see.
While the earth and the sky stand still
  forever
How swiftly changing time flies across
  man's face.
O you who sit over your full cup and do not
  drink,
Tell me, for whom are you still waiting?[1]

More than anything else I have ever read in
literature, these lines from Hermann Hesse's short
story, "Klingsor's Last Summer," capture the essence
of life's brevity. They say to me that life is short,
irrevocable, and transitory; therefore it must be lived
fully, not simply endured.

This quotation also tells me that I cannot afford
to wait until some later date to be happy, or to enjoy
and appreciate life. I must do it now because the
"now" of life is all I have for sure. The ever-sweeping
hand of time is flying across my face, taking with it
the youth that I once possessed . . . and what it takes
will never return. The days of my life seem to move
forward so rapidly that before I know it, my natal

days appear to be closer together. (I hadn't thought about it until now, but maybe that's why my friends rented a hearse for my last birthday. Instead of a joy ride, perhaps they were trying to underscore the fact that life is brief!)

One of the strongest recurring messages in the Word of God is that life is short—irreversible. In James 4:14 we read these words:

> Yet you do not know what your life will be like tomorrow. You are just a vapor that appears for a little while and then vanishes away.

Or as David says in Psalm 90, "soon life is gone and we fly away." You will also remember the famous list of life's appointed seasons found in Ecclesiastes 3, where Solomon refers to a time to be born and a time to die. In fact, that phrase is very short—one verse—as though that were indicative of the duration of life's span. All of the writings of history point up this characteristic of the life cycle: We are born, we live, then poof! . . . like a vapor, we vanish away.

Somehow we are not inclined to consider life's brevity when we're young, are we? We think we're going to last forever because we're strong, active, and all of life is stretching before us. As a teenager, I can remember, while reading the newspaper one day, coming across the Latin phrase, "sic transit gloria mundi," which I thought meant, "Gloria got sick on the bus Monday." How could I, as a kid, possibly understand anything about the glories of this world passing away? I was too young to have any comprehension of the meaning of loss. Hesse could never have written those words as a young boy. At the time he wrote that short story he was forty-two years old and had lost his home in the spoils of

war. His wife was mentally ill and he was a man
without belongings. A wanderer.

"So goes life," we say. "But what can we do about
it?" Well, obviously we can't stop time, and we cannot
prevent life from moving forward, but I think we can
do something which will cause the shortness of life
to work in our behalf, rather than against us. We
can give our lives away! As the commercial suggests,
we can "reach out and touch someone." Instead of
holing up in our own four-square world, we can strive
to be characterized by generosity. Listen to this from
the pen of the Apostle Paul:

> Be devoted to one another in brotherly
> love; give preference to one another in honor;
> not lagging behind in diligence, fervent in
> spirit, serving the Lord; rejoicing in hope,
> persevering in tribulation, devoted to prayer,
> contributing to the needs of the saints,
> practicing hospitality.   Romans 12:10-13

There's our word: Hospitality! And that's our calling
as it pertains to the art of giving our lives away.
Practicing hospitality.

Now, here comes the best part: Hospitality is a
natural opportunity for the unmarried person. It
follows the primary course of the single lifestyle. We
don't have to check with anybody if we want to
entertain a guest or guests. We don't have to have
fancy surroundings. We don't need to own a home.
We don't even need to have money. The only thing
that is required is a caring spirit. We do need that, or
we'll never reach out.

A single friend of mine who was a student some
years ago, and on a very limited budget, often had
guests in her tiny apartment for dinner—and she
didn't even own a set of pots and pans. The one pot

she had was a coffee pot. But with that vessel alone,
she demonstrated a great deal of panache in
entertaining guests. In it she cooked soups, eggs,
vegetables, and various hot beverages—one at a time,
of course, but each with smashing success. To be
invited to one of her meals was, in fact, an enviable
experience because everyone wanted to know what
she'd dream up next. She was extremely creative.

During the period of time she was in school, I
was living alone in an efficiency apartment. My
kitchen was so small that in order to open the oven
door I had to leave the room. It had been converted
from a walk-in closet to a cooking area, which I had
painted and decorated to suit my taste. My guests
and I had great times in that apartment and I recall
those occasions with the happiest of memories. The
size of one's home should never dictate the outreach
of one's heart.

In Lynn Shahan's best-selling guide for living on
your own, _Living Alone & Liking It_, there is a short
paragraph which in my opinion typifies the attitude
of invited guests. She says:

> Keep in mind that people love to be
> invited. They come without grand
> expectations, happy to have an evening
> away from their own surroundings.[2]

That is so true. People always like to be where the
action is. Often we are inclined to wait until
everything is copacetic before we reach out to anyone
else. We don't feel our living quarters are nice enough,
or finished enough, or furnished enough, or elaborate
enough. But people don't come to check us out. They
come to relax or have fun. And sometimes they come
because they are hungry for fellowship. Don't wait
until everything is perfect before you extend

hospitality. That day will never come.

Ney Bailey and Mary Graham, single roommates who are on the staff of Campus Crusade for Christ, lived for eight years at Lake Arrowhead, California, up the mountain from Crusade headquarters at Arrowhead Springs. They rented a home that belonged to a couple who resided elsewhere in the state. I can hardly remember a weekend last year when Ney and Mary were without houseguests. I finally asked them if they had any idea of how many people had visited them throughout the year. They thought for a minute, then told me around 350. On several occasions I had had the pleasure of being among that number; nevertheless, I found the idea of 350 guests hard to believe. That's almost one a day for the year! These women are not wealthy in a material sense either. Nor do they have time to spare. Ney and Mary are busy, active, involved working gals who travel a great deal and have just as many or as few hours in the day as you or I. But they have very caring spirits. Since their days of living at Lake Arrowhead, they have moved "down the mountain" into another dwelling. Do you know how many people were there for lunch on the day they moved in? Fifteen! No chairs. No table. No fancy meal. But an abundance of the ingredient needed for a generous lifestyle: hospitality.

I can think of four areas in my home life in which I have attempted to create a unique climate of hospitality toward others. If you would like, incorporate these in your outreach—but express them in your own style.

Use a Guest Book

This little volume is one of my most prized books. It sits quietly on my coffee table as a chronicle of the

thoughts and feelings of those who have visited in
my home. I started it eleven years ago, when I first
began living alone. My book also contains drawings,
greeting cards, labels, and a few maps, all done by
the hands of the contributors. But, most important, it
is filled with the spirit of individuals I love, enjoy,
and have entertained through the years—my parents
(both deceased now), my brothers, relatives; friends
from work, church, opera. Friends from the past and
present. Friends of other nationalities. Old friends.
Young friends. Children. Neighbors. It's almost as
though my life (at least for the past eleven years)
were recounted on its pages.

    Not only do people enjoy signing a guest book,
but they like reading it as well, and I love it. From
its pages I receive encouragement, cheer, laughter,
joy . . . and companionship. Mental images and voices
of past days.

Throw a Party

    Everybody loves a party! And practically
everyone I know gives parties and attends parties.
But the kind of gathering I refer to here is unique.
Dream up a new reason for celebrating—something
you've not done before. Then, develop your plans
and ideas around it, invite guests, and have fun!

    One of my favorite celebrations was a Christmas
party in May. May 23, 1968, to be exact. I was living
in Dallas at the time, with a roommate, and our
friend, Kurt, was living on the West Coast, having
moved there from Dallas two years before. He had
been traveling around the world on board ship as a
steward. That was his occupation. Because his
departure from Dallas had been prior to our usual
Christmas festivities, we had promised Kurt we'd
celebrate that holiday together upon his first visit to

Texas, thinking it would be in December, the month one normally celebrates Christmas.

However, when his letter came informing us he'd be arriving in Dallas during the month of May, laden with gifts from his various travels, we thought, "Why not? We'll celebrate Christmas now." So we did. We hung decorations, trimmed a pine tree that was donated by a gal in my office, wrapped gifts, made Christmas cookies, sang carols, roasted a turkey, played Christmas season recordings—in short, got completely into the holiday spirit. The decorated apartment and celebration became the talk of our friends and families, as well as the spectacle of the neighborhood. Someone even mailed us a Christmas card. It was a fabulous party. In fact, it lasted until about 4:00 A.M. if I recall. After all the festivities, we sat around the apartment, drinking coffee and listening to faraway tales spun from the lips of our erstwhile neighbor turned world traveler.

Never will I forget that party! It took a little effort but even that was pleasurable. One funny thing I remember that was unique to that celebration was the use of a beach towel in place of a tree skirt. By osmosis the water in which the tree was sitting traveled throughout the towel and dampened all the gifts. Nothing was ruined—just wet.

Unfortunately, those days were pre-guest book. If I had had the book then, just think of the spirit I could have captured to enjoy again and again. Alas!

Sing Some Songs

What is a home without music? And especially without group singing? Because I grew up surrounded by the sounds of music, participating almost daily in singing with my family, I love to sing and feel it is one of those nonessential attributes which enhances

*all social functions. And . . . one need not be able to
sing well to join in. That is totally unimportant. What
is important is letting our spirits go—entering into the
moment of collected friends spontaneously singing
together, with no thought of technique. Music in all
its forms is a potent vehicle of human feeling and
imagination.*

*This is an area of hospitality that is very common
in Europe. Everybody sings—in their homes, in their
shops, walking down the street, in restaurants, and
always among friends. It is a custom we Americans
would do well to adopt.*

Fly a Kite

*You may think this is a weird suggestion, but
flying a kite can be a very appealing and creative
way to share an afternoon. I rarely go on a picnic
without a kite and often, if I am planning the picnic,
I'll put one or two guests in charge of the kite. Julius
Karoblis, my dear European-born friend who lives in
northern California, makes marvelous kites, and if
he's among the group I always encourage him to bring
one of his creations. When America had her two
hundredth birthday in 1976, Julius made a kite to
celebrate that event, while Kurt and I made the
birthday cake . . . with two hundred candles, no less.
(It looked like a bonfire in a plate.) That kite was
red, white, and blue, with streamers and a long,
colorful tail. A magnificent reminder of the freedom
of America, made by a man who had moved to
America from Europe in order to enjoy that freedom.*

*Kite stories can be among the most enjoyable to
create . . . and relate. If you haven't flown a kite in a
while, go buy one (or better yet, make one); then pack
a picnic, invite a small group of your closest friends,
and take off to the hills or the sea—just to celebrate*

life.

However you choose to spend your leisure, always practice hospitality.

Klingsor did it in Hesse's short story, and at the close of the afternoon, spent with his dearest friends, as they danced down the sunlit road together, he said this:

> *. . . this day will never come again and anyone who fails to eat and drink and taste and smell it will never have it offered to him again in all eternity. The sun will never shine as it does today . . . you must play your part and sing a song, one of your best.*[3]

---

[1]Lines from *Klingsor's Last Summer* by Hermann Hesse, translated by Richard and Clara Winston. Copyright © 1970 by Farrar, Straus & Giroux, Inc. Reprinted by permission.

[2]Lynn Shahan, *Living Alone & Liking It* (New York: Stratford Press, 1981), p. 101.

[3]Hesse, *Klingsor's Last Summer*, p. 167.

Part Three

GOOD PERSONALITY–
Looking In

Have you ever played the game that begins with the words "What if . . .?" I'm sure you know the one. Here are a few of the typical questions:

What if this were your last day on earth . . . how would you spend it?

What if you could listen to only one more piece of music before you die . . . what would you hear?

What if you and two friends were marooned on an island for a month, and you could choose those friends . . . whom would you choose?

What if you were on death row and had to order the last meal of your choice . . . what would you order?

(I always loved getting that question because I knew immediately what I would say: A Greek salad, mushroom omelette with cheddar cheese, fresh broccoli, popovers, a bottle of Moët & Chandon Champagne, Zabaglione Trifle, and fresh ground Colombian coffee—as much as I wanted of all of it! I

*figured after that fabulous meal, I would be too full
to walk and they could just carry me down the hall
to the electric chair. What a way to go! And, if I were
really fortunate, maybe I would simply expire from
overeating.)*

*Occasionally, however, I got another "What if
. . .?" question that took a great deal more thought
and pondering: "What if you were going to be in
solitary confinement for one year and could take
only three books with you . . . what would you take?"
(Have you noticed how all my "What ifs . . .?" picture
such dire straits—"last day on earth," "marooned on
an island," "death row," "solitary confinement"? You'd
think I had been utterly deprived of any opportunities
for happiness in my life, would you not, by such
depressing frames of reference? Or that I have some
secret death wish. Neither could be further from the
truth. Actually, I am a very happy, contented person
for the most part; the reason I conjure up these
unlikely settings is that they produce the greatest
challenge for a creative response, and I think it's more
fun to toss around creative ideas.)*

*At any rate, there I was with this question about
books. I love books and I love to read, so to narrow
my "love list" of books down to only three was
practically impossible. I would rack my brain in an
attempt to determine which books would be worthy
of a year's investigation and companionship . . . all
the while remembering for each one I chose I'd have
to leave behind dozens of others. "Three? Only three?"
I'd ask. "Couldn't you make it ten or twenty? After
all, I've got a whole year." (This was serious
business!)*

*"Nope! That was the question and three was the
number. No more."*

OK. My first choice was always the Bible because,

being largely familiar with its contents, I knew it
would provide spiritual and emotional strength
during a time of possible hardship, loneliness, and
deprivation—as well as the fact that I would finally
have opportunity to read it without interruption or
distraction from the outside world.

The second volume chosen was the most recent
edition of Webster's Dictionary. I've always been
fascinated by words and language, and this book
would be a source of learning new words as well as
improving my vocabulary and spelling. Might as well
have a worthwhile project if I'm going to be stuck in
one spot for long.

Then, finally, the third precious book (my choices
were all gone now!) would usually be the one I was
reading at the time, so as not to leave it unfinished—
if it were really good, that is. Or some thick tome I
had always wanted to read but for which I had never
taken the time . . . something like Tolstoy's War and
Peace or Homer's The Iliad and The Odyssey, or
Dante's The Divine Comedy. Great books, all, but
time-consuming to read.

There they were, my three books, accompanying
me into this one year period of isolation. "Those are
good choices," I thought, "but are they the best
choices? Look at all those favorite, meaningful books
you had to leave behind." Then . . . I remembered it
was only a game, and I was glad.

Books are like friends . . . individual, unique,
and inestimable. They each contribute something
different yet valuable to our lives. They should be
chosen carefully, enjoyed lovingly, and given time to
grow on us. Reading brings us from darkness into
light, from ignorance to knowledge, from
imprisonment to freedom. By means of reading we
are better able to ferret out the meanings and

*possibilities of life. The voices of Reason, Victory,
Beauty, Faith, History, Poetry, Science . . . reach out
to instruct and encourage us from the author's pen,
and we are the better for it.*

*Books contain the power to lift us from the milieu
in which we live and work. It is as though they have
the capability of transporting us into another realm
of being. Emily Dickinson captured that very
thought.*

> *He ate and drank the precious words,
> His spirit grew robust;
> He knew no more that he was poor,
> Nor that his frame was dust.
> He danced along the dingy days,
> And this bequest of wings
> Was but a book. What liberty
> A loosened spirit brings.[1]*

*Reading acquaints us with the qualities of God
and humanity. It aids immeasurably in the building
of our characters as we pursue not only knowledge,
but a degree of excellence as well. Because of this
end result—that is, the building of character—I am
of the firm conviction that we should read . . . should
have a reading program of some type in our lives.
We need a self-imposed goal toward which we
consciously aim.*

*I believe that each person has a spiritual
obligation before God to learn how to live well, to
live fully, as opposed to knowing only how to live
comfortably. In a sense, I'm talking about an
academic program which improves the soul, and
directs it to God. A person cannot be taught courage,
tolerance, or dependability in the same way he or
she is taught geometry. Reading should create
associative thinking in us and it should provide*

criteria for determining what has meaning in our lives.

As we consider the world of academics, let's explore two avenues of thought regarding personal accountability in our pursuit toward excellence. The first avenue, and the more important of the two, is a reading program which will acquaint us with God—a knowledge of His abilities. Second, a program which will acquaint us with humanity—a knowledge of our responsibilities. I realize that in the broadest sense these are enormous pursuits, and I further realize that no matter the extent of our reading in either area, we will only scratch the surface of all that is available. Nevertheless, it is of paramount importance that we never stagnate mentally. There should never be enough hours in the day to read all we want to read!

In A. W. Tozer's excellent book, The Knowledge of the Holy, he said:

> We who live in this nervous age would be wise to meditate on our lives and our days long and often before the face of God and on the edge of eternity. For we are made for eternity as certainly as we are made for time, and as responsible moral beings we must deal with both.[2]

Our times can most assuredly be characterized by "this nervous age," but the range of knowledge we can accumulate and apply will, I believe, ease the pain and fear the nervousness produces. Therefore, I suggest a reading program as a venture which will expand both our intellectual and spiritual horizons.

At the outset, however, I want to emphasize something: Standing apart from all other books, of course, will be God's Word—the Bible. I cannot stress *earnestly enough the incomparable value of knowing scripture—reading it, meditating upon it, memorizing it, and applying it to our lives. It contains a power that no other book has. Nor can I encourage anyone too fervently to make a study of the doctrines of the Word of God. A knowledge of doctrine, coupled with memorized scripture, is our greatest spiritual treasure, apart from salvation itself. And whatever it takes to gain a knowledge of the written Word is worth the price.*

I am going to suggest a goal for each of the two categories as an end to keep in view. Following that will be a list of twelve books (in alphabetical order according to author), which have had the greatest value for me in reaching that goal. I offer all of this only as a suggestion, but by means of it I hope to encourage you to make up your own reading program, adding newly-discovered works year after year . . . to be read, savored, and assimilated into your life.

Lists, I know, are dangerous because they always omit someone's favorite. But they are also helpful in that they provide a springboard for thought. When any writer suggests a list of anything, there is the chance of overlooking material that should be included. Criticism will usually be directed toward the list maker. So, know at the beginning that these lists are not ex cathedra. They are not <u>the</u> lists, they are <u>my</u> lists. There's a difference. They are merely the writings which have supplied, for me, the richest source of growth, as well as those which have had the most profound effect upon my thinking thus far in life. If you don't agree with me, I won't be mad. But, before disagreeing too forcefully, read the work for yourself, then decide. Everyone must determine for him or herself which teachings will be the most beneficial in discerning the meanings and possibilities of life. There are, of course, hundreds of volumes from which one can choose. (What if we could only choose three?) The important thing is to read! And I promise you, as you follow your course of reading, a sense of mental expansion will illumine new areas of interest and thought which you never dreamed possible.

Oh! A final caution: In choosing books you read and want to apply in your life, you might use your "filter system" outlined in Chapter 2. Here is a good opportunity to screen what you read with the grid of discernment, keeping in mind what will profit you in spiritual and mental growth. The mature reader sees very quickly that discrimination is extremely important in reading anything.

But I also believe we need an open mind as we approach secular authors. Some people are so narrow in their thinking that they won't own a book that's not written by a professing Christian. That is a shame because there is a world of information—valid information—available, written by individuals who are not in our spiritual camp. So, open up your mind and heart to this venture. You will drink from the fountain of knowledge in direct proportion to your thirst.

God—A Knowledge of His Abilities
Suggested Goal, from the Bible, 1 Chronicles 28:9:

> . . . know the God of your father, and serve Him with a whole heart and a willing mind; for the LORD searches all hearts, and understands every intent of the thoughts. If you seek Him, He will let you find Him; but if you forsake Him, He will reject you forever.

Suggested Reading List:

1. *The Confessions of St. Augustine*
2. *Ethics*—Dietrich Bonhoeffer
3. *Pilgrim's Progress*—John Bunyan
4. *Mere Christianity*—C. S. Lewis
5. *Knowing God*—J. I. Packer
6. *Man's Problems—God's Answers*—Dwight Pentecost
7. *Robust in Faith*—Oswald Sanders
8. *The God Who Is There*—Francis Schaeffer
9. *True Spirituality*—Francis Schaeffer
10. *Basic Christianity*—John R. W. Stott
11. *The Strong and the Weak*—Paul Tournier
12. *The Knowledge of the Holy*—A. W. Tozer

Humanity—A Knowledge of Our Responsibilities
Suggested Goal, *from* <u>Report to Greco</u>, *by Nikos Kazantzakis:*

> *Nothing is certain. For that very reason every people, every individual, has a great responsibility in our amorphous, uncertain age, a greater responsibility than ever before. It is in such uncertain, possibility-filled times that the contribution of a people and of an individual can have incalculable value.*
>
> *What, then, is our duty? It is to carefully distinguish the historic moment in which we live and to consciously assign our small energies to a specific battlefield.*[3]

Suggested Reading List:

1. The Speeches of Winston Churchill
2. *Civilisation*—Kenneth Clark
3. *Crime and Punishment*—Fyodor Dostoevsky
4. *An American Tragedy*—Theodore Dreiser
5. *Interpretations of Life*—Will and Ariel Durant

6. *Markings*—Dag Hammarskjöld
7. *Scarlet Letter*—Nathaniel Hawthorne
8. *Report to Greco*—Nikos Kazantzakis
9. *Othello*—William Shakespeare
10. *Travels with Charley*—John Steinbeck
11. *Anna Karenina*—Leo Tolstoy
12. *The Power of Art*—John Warbeke

There are a few books which I enjoy so much, for the sheer beauty and poetry of their language and message, that I like to re-read them each year, if possible. But because they don't necessarily fit into either of the two above-specified categories, yet have had such a strong effect upon my aesthetic approach to life, I list them here separately for your consideration.

1. *Jane Eyre*—Charlotte Brontë
2. *The Complete Poems of Rupert Brooke*
3. *Alice's Adventures in Wonderland*—Lewis Carroll
4. *David Copperfield*—Charles Dickens
5. *Out of Africa*—Isak Dinesen
6. *Narcissus and Goldmund*—Hermann Hesse
7. *A Severe Mercy*—Sheldon Vanauken

People enjoy and appreciate books for many different reasons. Some, for simply the beauty of their bindings and art work; others, for age and monetary value. We all own books we treasure because they were gifts from people we love or respect. Books represent different periods of our life, different instructors, different stages of growth. In terms of content, we seek to be entertained, moved, taught, healed, even changed, by means of a book.

Personally speaking, the volumes to which I am primarily drawn are those which offer commentaries on social values. They address human dilemmas.

Sometimes they offer solutions to these situations,
but more often than not they simply pose questions
which make me think about my own life. Questions
such as these:

1. To what degree can we alter our circumstances by using our own free will?
2. Does the dream we have about life ever meet
   reality?
3. What do we actually mean when we say, "We
   are our brother's keeper"?
4. Can one live outside the moral precepts of
   society and survive? What is survival?
5. To what degree is one limited by one's
   environment and/or heritage?

These are the types of questions I love to ponder and
have pondered for years. Of course, there's no
absolute answer because each person must bring to
these questions his or her own experience, knowledge,
and background. Questions of this nature are relative
to different individuals in different circumstances.
They are among life's puzzles. But as I read accounts
of others also doing battle with these issues, I find I
am not alone in my search for life's meaning. It's a
universal dilemma.

Let me give you an example of a question I have
considered deeply for many years and how I have
finally received understanding of it as I have coupled
my experiences with what I have read from the pages
of literature. The question is, "How does one deal
effectively with grief?" We both know, you and I, that
this is a relative question and there is no perfect
answer to it. Its solution depends upon the person
dealing with the dilemma. Therefore, I don't
necessarily look for a solution in my reading, I look
for insight. I want to know if anyone else deals with

*this as I would. As I approach the subject, I ask
myself, "If there is no definite answer, then what is
the best course of direction to follow when I am forced
to deal with grief?"*

*I have read in the Old Testament of various saints
who suffered loss—who grieved deeply. Men like
Job, David, Jeremiah. Job even said if his grief were
weighed it would be "heavier than the sand of the
seas." How could he bear that degree of hurt or loss?
I have wondered. How does one do that in one's flesh?
I know Isaiah prophesied that Christ would bear all
our griefs—and I believe that, certainly. Or in the
New Testament there are references to one's bearing
up patiently under sorrow or grief. I know these truths
in my head, but living them out effectively is another
thing entirely. How do I do that? How am I able to go
on in life with a tremendously empty spot in my heart
that was once filled by someone I loved deeply? That's
the question.*

*I know, too, all the answers well-meaning
Christians give: "God is able. He knows your sorrow.
He will be with you in this." Or, "Just trust God. He
took your loved one in order to teach you something.
You must be strong and bear up under this." These
may be true concepts but they are often inappropriate
and I find most people resent them. It has been my
experience with people who are grieving that they
would much prefer the companionship of silence,
knowing someone is loving them and available, but
quiet.*

*Most of us have experienced grief in our lives at
one time or another: loss of a parent or both parents,
loss of a friend, the death of a spouse, perhaps, or
even a child. This is what I mean by a "universal
human dilemma." Either we have faced it or we will
face it during our lifetime. In an attempt to provide*

an example of how reading has aided me in my
search to deal with this problem effectively, I want to
tell you about a dear single friend of mine, Nancy
King, who, during a period of tremendous loss,
exemplified the truth of the insights I had read and
pondered regarding grief. I choose Nancy as my
example because of the unique circumstances
surrounding her loss. Her dearest friend (and
roommate), a twenty-nine-year-old single woman,
drowned while trapped in a car during the Big
Thompson Canyon flood.

   You don't know Nancy, perhaps, but she knows
you. She's aware of who you are because she is typing
the manuscript for this book. Nancy is a close, sweet
friend. We spend a great deal of time together as any
two people do who are working on a joint project. I
didn't know Nancy when her roommate drowned,
but I heard about it through mutual friends; and for
some unknown, inexplicable reason, I loved Nancy
before I met her, on the basis of that story concerning
her loss. My heart went out to her. I knew she was a
Christian, as was the friend who died in the flood,
and I thought about Nancy often in my effort to
comprehend the grief she must have endured during
that time.

   Later, Nancy and I met and became friends. In
time I asked her to tell me about losing someone so
dear to her. She opened her heart to me completely,
telling me the whole story of the warm, happy, loving,
fun relationship she had had with Barbie, and the
unalterable grief she experienced when Barbie was
taken by death.

   "You know, Luci," Nancy said, "I had never
experienced that degree of pain. It was agony—like
God was physically expanding my heart so it could
contain something that had never been there before.

*It hurt like nothing had ever hurt in my life." As I
listened to her, I thought of the words I had once read
by Leon Bloy:*

> *Man has places in his heart
>   which do not yet exist,
> And into them he enters suffering
>   in order that they may have existence.[4]*

*It fit exactly as Nancy was describing her pain.
She went on, "But I had to believe it. Barbie was gone.
There was no bringing her back. Although I couldn't
understand it and I hated it, I simply had to bear it.
I had no choice but to bear it. I knew God was with
me and would help me find meaning in it." I listened
carefully to every word Nancy said. But at the same
moment, my mind raced to that moving, gripping
chapter in* A Severe Mercy *where Sheldon Vanauken
spoke of his wife's death and having to deal with his
grief. I remembered his words:*

> *If I must bear it, though, I would bear
> it—find the whole meaning of it, taste the
> whole of it. I was driven by an unswerving
> determination to plumb the depths as well
> as to know the Davy I loved: to understand
> why she had lived and died, to learn from
> sorrow whatever it had to teach.[5]*

*Nancy continued, "I went through all of Barbie's
things, piece by piece, as though I were tenderly
caring for her. And with everything I touched I grieved
because I knew she was gone. Until we would one
day meet in heaven, I wouldn't see her again. I had
to reconcile within myself that she was no longer on
this earth except in my remembrance of her."*
*Wasn't that what Hermann Hesse said about
grief?*

*. . . The sacrifice of the dead must take
place in our own souls, through thoughts,
through exacting memory, whereby we
reconstruct the loved one within us. If we
can do this, the dead live on by our side,
their image is saved and helps to make our
grief fruitful.*[6]

*"Oh Nancy," I thought, "your account corroborates
everything I have ever pondered about grief. You
verify all that I've read and feel must be true. First,
that God expands our hearts to make room for it only
when He must. Second, that He causes us to bear
the pain only when we face the fact of the death and
determine to find meaning in both the living and
dying of the person we loved. Third, that we cannot
put grief entirely to rest until we live it out, letting it
flow completely through us, draining us, not running
away from it. And fourth, that we must make our
own personal study of what that particular individual
meant to us. Then, and only then, will our grief be
'fruitful' as Hesse said."*

*Nancy hadn't asked for that burden. She had
not wanted it nor had she deserved that degree of
suffering, humanly speaking. But she had no choice.
She loved Barbie; God took Barbie; and Nancy was
left with the pain. The world could say she was a
hapless victim in it all, that she was unlucky to have
this happen to her. But Nancy knew her inordinate
suffering was at the hands of a just and all-knowing
God. Her insufferable burden was given by a loving,
compassionate heavenly Father.*

*"It's OK now, Luci," she said in closing the subject.
"That happened over five years ago and I know Barbie
is with the Lord. Although the memory of her is etched
in my mind forever, I can go on without grieving*

anymore. I'm stronger because of the suffering. One day we'll meet again and that's what counts."

Sheldon Vanauken wrote in closing that poignant chapter:

> Some people run away from grief, go on world cruises or move to another town. But they do not escape, I think. The memories, unbidden, spring into their minds, scattered perhaps over the years. There is, maybe, something to be said for facing them all deliberately and straightaway.[7]

I received no absolute answers regarding this dilemma as Nancy unfolded her story to me, because I do not believe there are definite answers as such. However, the insights gleaned from her actual account bore testimony to the validity of my own reading and pondering of this common human dilemma. I felt I had learned something very valuable in terms of my quest toward knowing God, as well as understanding humanity. And I felt my soul had been improved—once again directed toward God.

Dealing effectively with grief is only one of many subjects we could have considered in this chapter. It is a noteworthy example, however, of one's responsibility in learning how to live fully. We are never too old to learn. Granted, our mental comprehension may be more astute at an earlier age, but the aging process should never keep us from growing or expanding our horizons. Anyone, at any age, can incorporate the personal program for education of which I have spoken in this chapter. The opportunity is now! Don't wait to begin. In Act IV of Shakespeare's play, Julius Caesar, there are seven poignant lines spoken by Brutus to Cassius which capture the importance of seizing opportunities.

> There is a tide in the affairs of men,
> Which, taken at the flood, leads on to
>   fortune;
> Omitted, all the voyage of their life
> Is bound in shallows and in miseries.
> On such a full sea are we now afloat,
> And we must take the current when it
>   serves,
> Or lose our ventures.[8]

Will it cost you? Oh yes! Everything of value costs something: time, money, or energy. Every prize has its price, and if we hope to obtain the prize, we must pay that price.

What if, in your lifetime, you wanted to gain the greatest amount of information possible regarding God's abilities and humanity's responsibilities, but you could only do that through reading the Bible and two dozen other books . . . which books would you choose?

> Men do not understand books until they
> have had a certain amount of life, or at any
> rate no man understands a deep book until
> he has seen and lived at least part of its
> contents.[9]
>
>   Ezra Pound

[1]Emily Dickinson, *Poems*, ed. Mabel Loomis Todd and T. W. Higginson (Cleveland: World Publishing Co., 1948), p. 47. By permission of Harper and Row, Publishers, Inc.

[2]A. W. Tozer, *Knowledge of the Holy* (New York: Harper and Brothers, 1961), p. 47.

[3]Nikos Kazantzakis, *Report to Greco* (New York: Bantam Books, 1965), p. 401.

[4]Louis M. Savary, S. J., *Listen to Love* (New York: Regina Press, 1968), p. 72.

[5]Sheldon Vanauken, *A Severe Mercy* (San Francisco: Harper and Row, Publishers, 1977), p. 187.

[6]Hermann Hesse, *Reflections* (New York: Farrar, Straus, and Giroux, 1974), p. 182.

[7]Vanauken, *A Severe Mercy*, p. 194-195.

[8]*Julius Caesar*, act 4, sc. 3, lines 217-223.

[9]John Bartlett, *Familiar Quotations*, ed. Christopher Morley (Boston: Little, Brown and Company, 1951), p. 934.

Chapter Eight —
Arts

Since childhood I have always had somewhat of a flair for theatrics. My family was extremely demonstrative and outgoing, and we entertained each other with our crazy antics. I suppose when there is no television in one's home, families are inclined to create their own floor shows. We certainly did that . . . all the time. But, being the "ham" that I was, I gained enough confidence in-house to take my performances elsewhere. That was a mistake!

I must have been seven or eight years old and was walking home from school one hot afternoon, carrying an armload of books, when I became bored with this daily routine. So I decided to act as though I were in a violent snowstorm, actually battling for my life. For some reason I went all out! What were once school books became a shield to protect my face from the sudden, unexpected blizzard. I held them in front of me as I staggered about, falling once or twice, all the while making howling wind noises with my mouth. For a full minute or so it seemed realistic, but at the height of this production, when I looked up to see how far I was from shelter, the corner of my eye caught a view of the neighbor's porch. Every member of the family was there, sitting in utter silence *staring at me, trying to comprehend what on earth had overcome the girl next door.*

I found myself wishing the ground would open and swallow me up, but it didn't. Just as their laughter broke the silence, fear gripped my senses. To say I was mortified would have been an understatement. I ducked my head and raced home. It was literally weeks before I wanted to appear in public again, and once more the ritual of walking home from school returned to all accepted standards of conformity. Never again was there a snowstorm on a hot afternoon in Texas!

Several years after that embarrassing episode, my parents enrolled me in private elocution lessons with a fine teacher in Houston who had had an active, successful career on the New York stage. I loved those classes and benefited from them greatly, I'm sure, even though initially Mother and Dad may have done it to save the family name.

What appeared to be a natural desire and fearlessness on my part, to be "on stage," received for the first time a professional touch and critique from one who actually had known success in the field. Not only was I a willing and eager pupil, but I gained the rudimentary knowledge needed for proper style in public speaking, a basic realization of one's need to be articulate, as well as voice control and projection. And I had a wonderful time! Betty Green Little, my teacher, had students of all ages. She worked with us in groups as well as individually, and our recitals consisted of public readings, characterizations, plays, debates, and occasionally extemporaneous speaking. We even studied voice inflection needed to express certain words. To this day I can say "Oh!" thirty-six different ways when called upon.

I would say that by virtue of my heritage, a tremendous love of the arts was probably inevitable. As far back into my life as I can draw up images, I envision my maternal grandmother, a piano teacher for thirty-three years, playing for either her own personal enjoyment or as accompaniment to the singing of her children and grandchildren. Also, my grandfather as a young man played trumpet in a small orchestra, I have been told. Both participated, through the years, in many church and civic music programs in the Texas town in which they lived, and together they fostered the love of music in each of their children.

One of my aunts—my mother's younger sister— while an artist by talent and education, is also an excellent pianist, and my mother loved to sing, majoring in voice during her college days. We often sang duets in church, she a soprano and I a contralto, and occasionally my two brothers joined us for quartets: Chuck, a tenor, and Orville, bass.

I can even recall, in the mothballs of my memory, scenes of the three of us as very young children, standing in stair steps on a drugstore counter, singing to the proprietor and local constituency for free ice cream cones. The more verses we sang, the more scoops we got! I think my father imagined us as the undiscovered von Trapp family replacements. He was utterly delighted to pack us off on these jaunts, always receiving verbal praise for his talented and fearless offspring. We sang for anybody who would listen and, as I remember, were completely at ease before an audience. It was fun, and after all, the goal of a double or triple decker cone gave us the incentive to sing every verse we had memorized.

When we were teenagers, I began to study voice while my brothers learned to play various musical

instruments. Orville, who at one time had aspirations
of becoming a concert pianist, began taking piano
lessons, and those continued for fifteen years. Chuck
learned to play clarinet, saxophone, oboe, and flute.
He was also quite active in school dramas, and
considered, for a short time, the theater as a possible
career. Even now he is adept at acting skills.

When I think back upon it all, I am acutely aware
of the financial sacrifice my parents must have made
to see that the three of us were exposed to a broad
spectrum of the fine arts at a very early age. In
addition to encouraging private enterprise in various
artistic expressions, they gave positive support to our
attendance at the Houston Symphony performances
through the school lyceum programs. We sang for
seven consecutive years in a city-wide production of
Handel's Messiah, under the directorship of an
excellent Handel interpreter and conductor. We
visited the Houston Art Museum regularly. In fact,
the arts exercised such a measure of influence and
control over our time and endeavors as a family, that
I believe it is accurate to say they had an enormous
amount to do with determining the quality and style
of my later life. For that one aspect of training alone
I will owe my parents and grandparents an eternal
debt of gratitude. Little did they realize that a
knowledge of and appreciation for the arts would
enhance the whole of my life.

What is it exactly that the arts provide which
affects the quality of a lifestyle? It is a bit difficult to
define in terms of its scope and importance because
the "art experience," while one of the most
spontaneously natural and pleasant expressions of
human life, is different to different people.
Fortunately, it is not just an esoteric pursuit for the
aesthete; it is, rather, "the province of every human

being." Art gives life color, richness, rhythm, fullness, and it makes us inventive, searching, more daring individuals. By its imaginative powers, art supplies character to our environment and beauty to our surroundings. Generally speaking, the arts add a charm to life, enhancing daily routine and making something beautiful or clever out of the ordinary.

Specifically speaking, participation in or the enjoyment of art intensifies our normal experience. It sharpens our senses, granting us the ability for more profound contemplation. And it softens our emotions, giving us more sympathy toward other people and toward life itself. In short, when the "art spirit" is alive in a person, that individual is interested in living, as well as interesting to other people.

And why is all of this so important? I'm glad you asked! The person who is imaginative in expression, sensitive to human feelings, in search of beauty, and creative in thought will be the person who is not only successful in living fully, but is able to enjoy quality leisure as well. There will rarely be boredom, dullness, or passivity.

I talk with single men and women so often who are unhappy, bored . . . dull. And I have never been able to understand why when there is so much to see, to read, to enjoy. But leisure time, unfortunately, can be the unmarried person's downfall. Therefore, quality leisure must be cultivated. One of the greatest advantages of living in a civilized culture is to have time for leisure—and the arts are leisure's best fruit.

In the enjoyment of leisure time, there are several areas which, throughout my life, have provided a source of emotional and mental well-being. These areas have been immeasurable in expanding my horizons, intensifying my regard for creativity, and increasing my appreciation of beauty and form. Next *time you have a free hour or evening to spend in leisure, why don't you listen to an album of music or go to a play? You might visit a local gallery, or perhaps try your hand at painting. If you're really adventuresome, attend an opera! Each of those fields has a world of pleasure in it. Consider them one at a time.*

Music

Leonard Bernstein once said,

> *I am a fanatic music lover. I can't live one day without hearing music, playing it, studying it, or thinking about it. And all this is quite apart from my professional role as a musician; I am a fan, a committed member of the musical public.*[1]

I too am a fan! An avid fan, and a day in my life without music is absolutely unheard of. Please don't get the mistaken idea that one need be only a classical music fan to be a "committed member of the musical public." Some evenings, depending upon my mood or taste, I only want to hear the jazz piano of Claude Bolling or the talented musicianship of Barbra Streisand. (I think I own every record she's made!) You see, taste has little to do with quality, since quality can exist in any style.

I would say the "music I live by" finds its nourishment in the ranks of classical compositions, from composers such as Brahms, Chopin, Vivaldi, Tchaikovsky, Puccini, Rachmaninoff, Verdi, Beethoven, etc. Nevertheless, I have grown in my appreciation of much popular music of today. For a number of years I must honestly confess I enjoyed only a very narrow band of music, but with exposure my tastes have broadened. Here's how it started . . .

At one time I lived next door to a young man who chose to play Simon and Garfunkel during the middle of the night. I would be awakened and lie in bed, trying to think of a tactful way to ask him to turn down the music. At first, I prayed for him and for his soul (which had to be unregenerate if he liked Simon and Garfunkel), in the hope that God would convict him of his thoughtlessness and relieve me of a verbal confrontation. I did this for two nights, but it didn't work. The music played on.

The third night, when my walls began to vibrate with "El Condor Pasa" and "Homeward Bound," I determined in my mind that I'd leave a note on his door the next morning, asking him to please be more thoughtful of his neighbors at that hour. So, as I left for work that day, I taped a kind, carefully worded note to his front door. That evening I found a note on my door. The neighbor apologized for his selfishness and said it wouldn't happen again. He closed by saying, "I am really sorry!—George." Well! It worked, and I was happy.

You can imagine my complete surprise when, during that very night, I once again heard "Bridge over Troubled Water" blasting through the stillness. What was it with that guy? This time, I decided to challenge him with a musical duel. I got up, went to my stereo, and turned on, full blast, Carmina Burana by Carl Orff, which combines huge vocal forces at the very beginning of the work. It's enough to knock you out of your concert chair, much less out of bed in the wee hours of the morning. I played it for three or four minutes, then cut it off. There was no sound . . . Carmina Burana had quit but so had Simon and Garfunkel. Finally! I marched off to bed, triumphant.

The following day when I got home from my office,

I found a new note from George. He said he had not meant to be rude, but that he worked late and the only time he had to listen to his music was from midnight on. He once again apologized for not being a better neighbor and announced he was moving. Then the note said, "By the way, what was that you were playing last night on your record player? It was beautiful. I'd like to buy it." I had to laugh at the incongruity of it all.

He did move shortly after that and, ironically enough, I missed Simon and Garfunkel. Would you believe I went out and bought that recording! I had grown, despite my own musical inflexibility, to like their music and their message. And I've always wondered if George ever bought <u>Carmina Burana.</u>

That episode, upon reflection, made me see how easy it was to get in a rut, musically, and stay there. I admit, if I had heard Simon and Garfunkel under more normal listening conditions, perhaps my mind would have been open to their style of music—but I doubt it. I always tuned out "that kind" of music.

However, being somewhat forced into listening in the middle of the night, my tastes expanded. I even found myself sincerely regretting that I had, at an earlier time, refused to sing, "We've Only Just Begun," for a friend's graduation because it was "beneath my taste." I had been wrong—critical. And I was sorry.

The "art experience" is different to different people. And we cannot judge taste for another, claiming there is no quality. Quality can exist in any style.

While I have your attention, will you please allow me a five-minute digression on the subject of opera? For those of you who have never listened to or seen opera, you have missed a monumental occasion in

*your musical experience. Utterly entertaining. Opera
is the most perfect combination of all the arts: ballet,
singing, orchestration, theater, lighting, costuming,
painting, architecture. For fifteen years I had the
happy privilege of being a member of the Dallas Civic
Opera Chorus, and I cannot tell you the numerous
avenues of excitement and opportunity which that
experience opened for me. I sang with the finest voices
in the world, under the leadership of opera's best
conductors and stage directors. I studied other
languages. I met exciting, interesting, unique
people—many of other nationalities in whose homes
I was a guest when traveling abroad. And I learned
music and staging that is vastly different from all
other choral work.*

*Some years ago I asked the aging mother of a
dear friend of mine if she liked opera and her answer
was classic. She said, "No, Luci. To me it's just
educated screeching!" I loved that answer because it
captured in very natural terminology the essence of
how most people judge opera. It's a common
judgment, but an unfortunate one, I'm sorry to say.
Tolstoy even said of opera, "People do not talk that
way." And he's right. We don't.*

*But what opera does is to provide a beautiful,
musical extension of human faculties. It gives us a
chance to sing feelings that are often too deep or subtle
to be said. Music serves as the bridge for those
feelings. Besides, opera is a lot of fun to attend—a
very real reason to dress to the teeth and look our
spiffiest. Give it a try—with an open mind!*

*Before I close the subject of music, let me add
this: I am frequently asked to suggest a list of classical
records for someone who wants to start a collection
but doesn't quite know where to begin. Therefore, for
those of you who want such guidance and find my*

taste in keeping with yours, here's that list.

6 Symphonies:

Beethoven — Symphony No. 3, E Flat Major,
— Op. 55 (<u>Eroica</u>)

Brahms — Symphony No. 3, F Major,
Op. 90

Dvořák — Symphony No. 9, E Minor,
Op. 95 (<u>New World</u>)

Mahler — Symphony No. 2, C Minor
(<u>Resurrection</u>)

Rachmaninoff — Symphony No. 2, E Minor,
Op. 27

Tchaikovsky — Symphony No. 6, B Minor,
Op. 74 (<u>Pathétique</u>)

6 Piano Concerti:

Brahms — Concerto for Piano & Orchestra,
No. 1, D Minor, Op. 15

Delius — Concerto for Piano & Orchestra,
C Minor

Grieg — Concerto for Piano & Orchestra,
A Minor, Op. 16

Rachmaninoff — Concerto for Piano & Orchestra,
No. 2, C Minor, Op. 18

Saint-Saëns — Concerto for Piano & Orchestra,
No. 2, G Minor, Op. 22

Tchaikovsky — Concerto for Piano & Orchestra,
No. 1, B Flat Minor, Op. 23

6 Violin Concerti:

Beethoven — Concerto in D Major for Violin &
Orchestra, Op. 61

Brahms — Concerto in D Major for Violin &
Orchestra, Op. 77

Bruch — Concerto No. 1, G Minor for
Violin & Orchestra, Op. 26

Dvořák — *Concerto in A Minor for Violin &*
Orchestra, Op. 53
Mendelssohn — *Concerto in E Minor for Violin &*
Orchestra, Op. 64
Tchaikovsky — *Concerto in D Major for Violin &*
Orchestra, Op. 35

6 Miscellaneous Works:
Beethoven — *Two Sonatas for Piano: Sonata*
No. 7, D Major, Op. 10, No. 3
Sonata No. 23, F Minor,
Op. 57
Brahms — *Sonata No. 3, D Minor, Op. 18*
Handel — *The <u>Messiah</u>*
Pachelbel — *Canon in D Major for Strings*
and Continuo
Poulenc — *Concerto for Two Pianos and*
Orchestra, D Minor
Vivaldi — *<u>Four Seasons</u>, op. 8, No. 1-4*

Just for fun and if needed in the middle of the night:
Orff — *<u>Carmina Burana</u>*

Drama

Schopenhauer said that the stage offers the perfect mirror of life. There is probably no other art form in which we see ourselves more clearly or can identify more readily. From the ancient Greek to the twentieth century, theater has given humanity its opportunity to recreate life's experiences—the good and bad, strong and weak, wise and foolish, delightful and painful. Drama holds a mirror up to human behavior, and as we view that drama on stage, it is as though we are looking at ourselves. Therein lies its power and longevity.

Did you ever attend a play which was so moving and engrossing that you felt you were riveted to your

*seat? And after it was over you continued to sit there,
dumbfounded? I have. In fact, that's my favorite kind
of theater—where my whole being is involved and
absorbed with the plot, the characters, the story.
Then, when I finally am able to get up, with my mind
still reeling from the experience, not only do I feel
I've gotten my money's worth, but I also feel enriched,
lifted . . . almost "blessed." A well-done film can do
the same for me, although my personal preference is
legitimate theater.*

*There are times, of course, when one simply
wants to be entertained, where there is no
requirement for an emotional response. In that case,
theater also has value. But the drama to which I am
basically referring is that which grips, then moves
my spirit . . . after which I am more aware of and
sympathetic toward human problems, as well as
acutely in tune with my own.*

*Why do I like that? I've pondered that question
from time to time, and I believe the true answer lies
in the fact that even though I cannot always
comprehend reasons for my own behavior, if I see
the same action in someone else, it helps me
understand the why of that behavior in myself. It
helps me to know myself. Dramatic art, as I said
earlier, gives expression to the whole gamut of human
life, and it presents, for our contemplation, life's
corruption and its health, its commonplaceness and
distinction. It aids in separating the important from
the insignificant. To put it simply—good theater
leaves me with a whole cluster of value judgments
about myself.*

*Why is that important? Because knowing myself
is important in how I face life. How I respond to what
life deals me. Do you recall in Chapter 3 where I
referred to the value of knowing one's patterns? Well,*

*one of the avenues of knowledge of one's patterns,
believe it or not, is witnessing drama on stage. I can
think of dozens of occasions when I have attended
theater and, upon leaving, have been moved to
positive action regarding some problem in my life at
the time, as a result of seeing myself in that
experience.*

*Certainly there is an awesome ability in a
playwright to produce such a vehicle for inspiration—
that, in itself, is the mystery of genius. Nevertheless,
the by-product of that ability finds its achievements
in a great deal more than affirmative ballyhoo. Good
plays can change lives. Or if you find that statement
too dogmatic, at least they can greatly alter behavior,
because by means of them we see ourselves as we
truly are.*

*That's what mirrors are for, aren't they, to aid us
in making effective changes in the areas of our lives
that need changing? Surely the Apostle James had
that same thought in mind when he wrote,*

> For if anyone is a hearer of the word and
> not a doer, he is like a man who looks at his
> natural face in a mirror; for once he has looked
> at himself and gone away, he has immediately
> forgotten what kind of person he was. But
> one who looks intently at the perfect law, the
> law of liberty, and abides by it, not having
> become a forgetful hearer but an effectual
> doer, this man shall be blessed in what he
> does.   James 1:23-25

Painting

*Being an ardent admirer of Winston Churchill
has led me to read a great many of his works. Among
my favorites is a beautifully written essay on the
subject of painting: "Painting As a Pastime," he calls*

it. It is clever and witty as well as profound—very characteristic of all his writing. In the essay, Churchill is attempting to get his reader involved in a hobby, any hobby that will take his or her mind off daily routine and stress. "Broadly speaking," he says, "human beings may be divided into three classes; those who are toiled to death, those who are worried to death, and those who are bored to death."[2] His hobby, painting, aided him in putting off death for ninety years!

What's your hobby?

The year prior to getting my degree in Art (twenty-six years ago . . . ugh!) I attended a summer school program at the University of Houston in order to get a couple of courses out of the way prior to the fall semester. I needed a general psychology course for sure, and I decided a class in oil painting would give a good balance: I could paint for three days of the week, then on the other two, spend my time determining why I painted what I did! It would be fun, and I would be accomplishing a goal as well.

I signed up for the painting class, knowing I had a small measure of talent, although it would be doubtful that any of my work would ever hang in the Louvre. On Monday, Wednesday, and Friday of each week I packed up my paint box, grabbed my palette and brushes, flung a camp stool over my shoulder, and went off to fight a battle between canvas and landscape. I didn't always win the battle, but I always fought a good fight and came home relaxed and refreshed.

For the first time in my life I learned many things. Painting was not just applying paint to a surface; it was seeing things in a new light. It was becoming aware of the relative value of other things that surrounded my subject: color, line, form, shading, shape, expressions. I went crazy with discovery, much like a photographer with a camera. There was never going to be enough time to learn all I wanted to about this wonderful, exciting new world. I painted all the time! On Tuesdays and Thursdays in Psychology, instead of trying to determine why I painted what I did, I spent my leftover energies in pondering how I would ever pass that course. I barely did. I made a D, and in looking back I have thought my professor probably gave me the grade because I was so rarely in class.

That summer course in oil painting, however, did more than improve my technique. It made me more imaginative, more interested in details, more patient in my desire to achieve results. And it made me more contemplative about nature and people. I became aware of faces and their expressions, hands, body movement. Much that I had taken for granted earlier was now a study in art. That course launched me into what has become a lifelong search for and appreciation of the creative inventiveness of people. It has set me free from preconceived ideas about what should constitute beauty, and it helped me form my own opinions regarding what has value and worth.

When I stand in front of the work of a great master of art—let's say, a Rembrandt painting—I am aware that even with my modicum of knowledge and experience as a dilettante, I can more fully appreciate and understand what I am viewing.

What was once a consuming desire for me to paint every day has been tempered into a creative, enjoyable hobby. I'm glad. I don't need to express myself that passionately anymore, but there are times when the avenue of painting is my only key to expression—more so than singing or drama. Then the old skills come back to me! Of course, I never got

*my paintings to hang in the Louvre . . . but neither
did Churchill.*

*There you have it: my rather abbreviated view of
the value of the arts in a person's life; a cursory look
at why I feel they are important. They transform much
of the routine of living into sources of joy, making our
humdrum, commonplace, ordinary days into creative
adventures. An awareness of the gifts of music,
painting, and drama not only enriches us, as God's
children, but gives us limitless opportunities for
continuous praise to our Heavenly Father.*

*On the curtain of Ford's Opera House in
Baltimore, Maryland, these words are painted—the
ultimate in artistic expression:*

> *God conceived the world, that was poetry;*
> *He formed it, that was sculpture;*
> *He colored it, that was painting;*
> *He peopled it with living beings;*
>   *that was the grand, divine, eternal*
>   *drama.*[3]

[1]Leonard Bernstein, *The Infinite Variety of Music*
(New York: Simon and Schuster, 1966), p. 10.

[2]Winston S. Churchill, *A Man of Destiny,*
(Waukesha, Wisconsin: Country Beautiful
Foundations, Inc., 1965), p. 64.

[3]John Bartlett, *Familiar Quotations,* ed.
Christopher Morley (Boston: Little, Brown and
Company, 1951), p. 508.

Chapter Nine — Associates

Do you remember the jocular friend of whom I spoke in Chapter 5, Marilyn Meberg? The person who made the play on words of the Rachmaninoff "preclude"? Well, there's more—much more to this individual, in terms of our association. Being the bright, sharp, educated woman that she is, Marilyn has a very serious side, but her personality is probably best described as a cross between that of Erma Bombeck and Carol Burnett. Crazy. Daring. Adventuresome. One who lives on the cutting edge of life. I have laughed at Marilyn and with Marilyn more often and more heartily than with any other person in my entire life—and believe me, I laughed a lot before we ever met. In my opinion, she is truly funny, evoking humor everywhere she goes.

But one of the pleasing things about this side of her personality is that she too laughs. She picks up on other people's humor quickly and does not require center stage. In other words, she not only produces and creates funny situations, but appreciates and responds to them as well. An appealing trait in an individual.

Marilyn teaches English at a local university and has a facile mind with a marvelous command

of the English language—but at times even that, too,
can be funny. Her quick wit, coupled with her verbal
expressions, often make her sound like a female
Charles Dickens. I love it! One morning I simply said,
in my own style, "Mar, how ya' doin'?" To which she
replied, without a moment's thought, "I am perfectly
content—as content, that is, as one can be, living in
an imperfect world and in a body whose days are
numbered." All right!! When I responded with a
guffaw she immediately saw the verbosity of her
answer and laughed herself. I've been tempted to
have that statement printed on a T-shirt for her as a
birthday gift, because, you see, that is true of any of
us at any point in our lives. Could one call that
profound humor?

Marilyn and I had been friends for only a matter
of months when she suggested that she introduce me
to her favorite city—Palm Springs. Each of us had
several hours free without other obligations, and I
was thrilled with the idea. At this point I had only
heard of Palm Springs as the laid-back, casually
elegant, always sunny, monied resort of the jet set.
Naturally I was eager to see for myself how that type
lived; so off we went to this California camelot.

For those of you who know the city, you'll agree
that it's a place with which almost everyone falls in
love, especially in the fall and winter when the
temperature is ideal. The shopping area is clean,
elegant, well arranged; no one is in a hurry. A very
mellow place, in my opinion. There are many good
restaurants, and in dining there one is apt to
encounter a celebrity at the next table.

After our day of soaking up the sun, window
shopping, and enjoying one another's company, we
decided to have dinner at an Italian restaurant on
the main drag called "Banducci's." Maybe you know

the establishment. It's a nice place—attractive decor,
reasonably priced, and the food is good. The dining
room is lined with photographs of famous
personalities, primarily Hollywood stars. But in every
picture there was also a blond-haired woman whom
neither of us recognized as anyone famous.

After we had been seated for a few minutes and
questioned between ourselves who she might be,
this very woman came into the restaurant, apparently
from the kitchen. She was well-groomed, tall, smiling.
I immediately recognized her as the same person in
the photographs. "Hey, Marilyn," I said, "look. There's
that woman in all these pictures. I'll bet that's Ms.
Banducci. What do you think?" Marilyn agreed. For
some reason it seemed to satisfy us to equate her as
both the owner and the individual who was
apparently acquainted with all those famous people.

Marilyn and I settled into a comfortable
conversation about things in general, ordered our
meal, and relaxed as we listened to the soft music of
a piano wafting across the dining room from a lounge
somewhere behind us, obscured by a partition.
Momentarily, Marilyn looked me straight in the eye
and said, "Luci, do you like bets?"

"I love bets, Marilyn," I said. "All my life I've
enjoyed a good bet, but I haven't always found
someone as daring as I am, so I usually squelch my
wacky ideas before they are expressed. If you like
bets, we're going to get along just fine." She assured
me that I had met my match. Then she asked me if I
wanted to make a bet with her. Enthusiastically I
agreed, and these were her terms:

1. Each of us was to guess the sex, hair
   color, and approximate age of the pianist
   —the person we could not see, but whose

> *pianistic ability we were enjoying.*
> 2. *Whoever got the majority of those facts right was the winner.*
> 3. *The loser had to do the bidding of the winner, no matter what.*

Met her match, indeed! I jumped at the idea. Understand, neither of us had ever been to this restaurant. It was our first time there and we knew nothing of the pianist, obviously. I told her I knew it was a woman, about fifty, blond, lots of hair; in fact, she probably looked a great deal like Ms. Banducci.

"No way," Marilyn said. "That's the playing of a man, I'm sure. Strong. Forceful. He's rather bald, with a fringe of black hair, and somewhat overweight. Besides, I'd recognize bald fingers anywhere! I know I'm right. Go look."

I hopped up, marched into the lounge—and I could hardly believe my eyes. There sat a fat man, balding (but with a small amount of black hair), playing the piano beautifully. When I returned to the table I announced to Marilyn that she was exactly right, followed by muttering something like, "I'll bet you've been here before." Laughingly, she assured me she hadn't, and the gleam in her eye indicated that her mental wheels were beginning to crank out what would be the best way to pay off this ludicrous bet.

Our food came and we began to eat. I changed the subject, hoping she would forget she had won. But all of a sudden she said, "I've got it. Oh! This is <u>great</u>. I've GOT it!" I stopped chewing, fearful of asking the sixty-four thousand dollar question: What? Then she said, "Now you promised that the loser would do the bidding of the winner, right?"

"Right!"

"And no matter what, you will do it, right?"

"Right, Mar. I'll do it. What in the world can be that insane?" (She was almost prostrate in the booth, laughing.)

"All right, Luci, here's what I want you to do: When we get ready to leave here tonight, you go up to that woman we think is Ms. Banducci, introduce yourself, and say to her, very seriously, 'Ms. Banducci, my chihuahua is so much better. Thank you for your prayers.' "

"WHAT!? Are you crazy, Marilyn? You've lost your mind! Nothing in the world could make me do such a ridiculous thing. She'll think I'm nuts."

"Of course she will. That's the whole point," she said between shrieks. "But you promised— remember? You said, 'No matter what.' "

Well, I was sick. I could hardly finish my meal. At the same time, I was in hysterics. It was terrible. I tried practicing my lines on Marilyn and she too was hysterical. I'm sure the clientele wondered what could possibly be so funny in our booth. The nearer time for our departure came, the sicker I got, but I knew there was no way out. I realized Ms. Banducci would never see me again (no question about that fact!) and I simply had to do it. Never had I had such a challenge in a bet. Not only had I met my match, but this would be my first, last, and only bet with Marilyn Meberg, because I was certain I would die of heart seizure right in front of Ms. Banducci.

We finished. I had dragged out eating as long as I possibly could, but one does finally come to the end of any meal. We stood up to go and I had our money to pay the check. My stomach was in knots. Ms. Banducci, being the gracious hostess that she appeared to be, was near the cash register, visiting with a table full of respectable-looking people. I asked

Marilyn to please wait outside, to which she quietly responded out of the side of her mouth, "Wild horses could not wrench me from your side!" I was doomed. My hour had come!

When Ms. Banducci turned away from her other guests she saw me and flashed a big smile. I cleared my throat.

"Are you Ms. Banducci?"

"Well yes, I am."

(A very attractive lady, who I'm sure thought I was going to say I was Elizabeth Taylor's sister, bringing her greetings from her old friend.) Instead, I very slowly, deliberately said, "Ms. Banducci, I'm Luci Swindoll and my friend and I are here from Fullerton for a visit." I stopped momentarily, hoping for a miracle of deliverance, as she continued to smile in a slightly mesmerized state, hanging on my every word. Then I continued, "Before we leave here, Ms. Banducci, I wanted to tell you—my chihuahua is so much better. Thank you for your prayers."

I'm not sure what I felt at that moment, but whatever it was, I hope to never feel it again as long as I live. It was a combination of utter agony for myself, a desire to murder the person I had come with, and fear that poor, innocent Ms. Banducci would throw a net over my head. Gradually, simultaneously, however, two things occurred: First, the smile that had crossed her face turned into that look one gets when one is hard of hearing but eager to perceive what has been said; and second, her hands left her sides and rested on my shoulders, with her eyes holding me in a puzzled gaze. Then, hesitatingly, she whispered, "Honey . . . you and your friend come back."

"Oh, we will, Ms. Banducci. We certainly *will," I lied. I paid the check and walked outside to find*

Marilyn reeling down the sidewalk, hardly able to catch her breath, she was laughing so uncontrollably. Absolutely beside herself!

I don't believe I have ever been as embarrassed nor as tickled at the same time. We sat in the car for at least fifteen minutes before we were able to drive away, laughing hysterically, reliving that unique, wacky experience, and trying to imagine what Ms. Banducci must be thinking at that moment. To this day, we laugh about that episode. And would you believe Marilyn has offered to buy my dinner if I'll go back into that restaurant sometime and tell Ms. Banducci my chihuahua died? What price friendship!

That's a good question: What price is friendship? What are you willing to pay in order to have friends, and what are you willing to pay to keep them? Threaded throughout this book is the theme that everything of value has a price. It costs you something in terms of time, money, or energy. And friendship is certainly of value—one of life's most valuable gifts.

I have had many years to think about the meaning of friendship, especially its tremendous importance to the single person, and I believe there are definite ingredients that give friendship its value. True friendship cannot be assessed overnight. It takes a long time to determine what ingredients are best between friends. The tests of time, separation, misunderstanding, differences, or aging cannot alter true friendship. These tests only make it stronger if there is real caring and investment.

Having friends adds such sweetness to life. "Friendship is tenderness," Emerson says. We all want to be close to someone who is tender toward us. Understanding. Loving. Kind. When we receive those qualities from others, it generally makes us more that way ourselves. Tenderness rubs off, doesn't it?

Now that I've lived over half my life, have had friends, have hurt and disappointed friends, have been hurt and disappointed by friends, and have experienced much of what it takes to maintain friendship, I think I am finally able to make some valid statements regarding its value and worth. I only wish I had known these principles when I was first starting out in life. That knowledge would have saved me a great deal of heartache. Alas! It's taken me a long time to learn these lessons. (And some of them I'm still learning.)

While your relationships may generally be characterized by congeniality and conviviality, I'll bet my bottom dollar that if they have any length or depth to them at all, there have been occasions where you wanted to give up; where you wanted to throw in the towel because of the difficulties involved in friendship. I certainly have felt that—many times. Sometimes human relationships are downright impossible. You know it and I know it. At that point, we have to weigh the circumstances, re-evaluate the priorities for the friendship, and determine if it's still worth the price.

Here are my six basic priorities for friendship: communication, acceptance, reciprocity, freedom, kindness, and mutuality. I want to comment on each one so you'll understand why I look for these particular ingredients in people. A few of my friends have all of them in abundance. Others have some of them. But unless there is at least one of these commodities in a person's makeup, I will probably not be drawn toward friendship. I would never be rude, of course, nor indifferent, but my spirit would not respond sufficiently to the other person, and there

would be no foundation stone on which to build a
friendship.

Communication

One of my favorite avocations in life is sitting
with a friend and the two of us "tracking together." It
is vital to my soul! If I have heard it once, I've heard
Marilyn ask me hundreds of times, "How are you in
your soul?" Unfortunately, that question scares some
people away, but it delights me. It makes me want
to reveal my heart—my joys, my hurts, my hopes,
my fears. It is therapeutic on many occasions,
relieving the tension and stress that has built up
inside me. Marilyn and I spend hours like this—she
talks and I listen to her, then I talk and she listens.
It's not structured. We each try to hear what the other
is saying—both verbally and non-verbally—then we
comment or laugh or advise or pray, or do whatever
the Spirit dictates. But it's free and it's wonderful.
She is a communicator who has no peers.

I never say we "share," because I don't like the
word share. It's grossly overworked among Christians.
And it implies that if I tell you something, you must
tell me something and maybe you don't want to.
Maybe you just want to sit there and listen. One can
"track" without speaking but one can't share without
speaking. That's why I prefer the term "tracking
together."

Communication is essential for growth in a
friendship. In the first place, we owe it to our friends
to define where we are with them—define the
perimeters of where we stand. I'm not implying that
the prerequisite for being a friend with someone is to
say to them, "Now look, here's the deal: You'll never
be my No. 1 friend. I like you a lot but that spot is
taken. In fact, we'll never be close. If you want to be

*friends with me you'll have to be content to remain
on the periphery of my life, etc." No. I don't mean
that. I mean sometimes there are cases of unrequited
friendships—friends who want more from us than
we are able or willing to give. In that instance, we
need to explain to them where they are in our life.
Be tactful and kind, but be honest. They will
appreciate it and, believe me, it will save you both a
great deal of grief down the road. Oh, the times I have
promised more than I could deliver, simply because I
didn't want a confrontation! I do that differently now
because I've learned to care more about their feelings
than my own. You don't want to offend your friends,
you just want to make them aware of the truth. Tell
them in the manner you would like to be told. As the
adage says: "Do you know how to keep from stepping
on other people's toes? Put yourself in their shoes."*

*In the second place, communication keeps the
friendship healthy. It not only apprises us of where
we stand, but it illumines the trouble spots by
providing an avenue to work on difficult areas or
differences until they are made acceptable to both
parties. Or, if all has been said and acceptability
has not been reached, it gives foundational grounds
to "agree to disagree." I find, in my relationships,
even if my ideas are rejected, I feel better if I know
they have been heard and at least considered and
understood. It is so important to be understood.
Understanding builds unity and harmony in
relationships.*

*In the third place, no one has all the answers to
any problem, especially interpersonal relationship
problems. Therefore, the vehicle of communication
gives us a chance to gain new insight by listening to
the suggestions of others, and by hearing our own
thoughts formed into words and ideas.*

Communication is a valuable skill to cultivate. I cannot recommend it highly enough as the basic key to friendship's longevity.

Acceptance
Accepting others as they are is a perfect picture of seeing theory lived out into practicality. We may say we accept others, but until we actually do it, it is only theory. No one can actually change anyone else, so why do we try so hard? Present to them the gospel? Yes! Attempt to introduce them to Christ? Fine. Suggest a better way of life or standard of living? They'll probably appreciate it. But change them? No. We can't do it. Our influence may have a positive effect on our associates, and there may be some changes as a result of that, but becoming friends with someone in order to change him or her doesn't work. It doesn't work in a marriage either.

I am learning that if we want our associates to change, two things must occur: We must leave their alteration to the work of God—to His Spirit and timing; and we must accept them (preferably love them) as they are. Acceptance has an important side effect, too, related to honesty or openness. If I know I am going to be accepted by another person, no matter what I say or do—if I know that I will not be judged for my behavior or comments—then I am more apt to be transparent with them. In fact, I will be open only to the degree that I know I'm going to be accepted. The less judgmental we are, the more easily other people will open their hearts to us. Correct? If I can show my vulnerabilities, fears, insecurities, and sensitivities to another individual and not be criticized or judged for them, I will feel that I can truly be myself. Here's a case in point.

Sophia and I are basically different. She is

younger than I am. She holds political, cultural, and theological views that are not only different from mine, but in some cases diametrically opposed. I'm American and she is Greek—living in Athens. She is fluent in five languages, and at times I feel I am barely fluent in one.

But in spite of our differences, no two friends could be closer nor love one another more than we. Throughout the twelve years of friendship we have had together, God has knit our hearts into a very strong and enduring bond. We have suffered with each other through the loss of my mother and both of our fathers, the deaths of her aunt and one of her dearest friends whom I also knew and respected, major surgeries, a formidable earthquake in her homeland, a change of locations and jobs (to name a few). Through them all, we have not only remained intimate friends, but grown closer. I have a strong emotional allegiance to Sophia and her family, and that allegiance only grows with the passing of time.

This relationship with my Greek friend that I prize so dearly has, for the most part, been built on two of my friendship priorities: communication and acceptance, and those, surprisingly enough, from over seven thousand miles apart. I have kept every letter, card, telegram, and note that Sophia has sent me and they number over five hundred. She has always remembered my birthdays and Christmas with a gift (and never been late, I might add), and she has repeatedly demonstrated her love to me and her acceptance of me in a thousand ways. When I visit her in Greece, we hardly have to catch each other up on our lives, because we stay current.

We could easily judge one another on important issues over which we differ, but why? Why should we spend our time trying to change each other? I respect Sophia's viewpoint and she respects mine. She's a highly intelligent, sensitive, generous person, and God has blessed the relationship we enjoy. It's easy to love her as she is, because she loves me as I am.

Reciprocity

About four years ago I experienced the need to "get away from it all." I wanted to go someplace where I would have no hassles—preferably a desert island. At the time, I was working through a problem in my life in which I needed a lot of time to think, re-evaluate, pray, and relax. A complete change of scenery. Since the desert island was not an option, I decided to visit one of my dearest friends in Texas, Judy Jacobs, who lives in a large, spacious home. I called Judy and proceeded to invite myself over for the Thanksgiving holidays! True to the gracious person she is, Judy seemed extremely pleased to have me come. She would meet my plane and was expansive in her generosity. "Certainly, I'd love to have you visit, Luci," she said. "There's always a place for you here, and we'll include you in our Thanksgiving dinner. Can't wait to be with you."

Her kindness relieved my mind of the fear I had about imposing on her and her family over the holiday. I arrived and felt very at home there. I took long walks or sat in front of the fireplace, thinking. Never once did Judy interrogate me to know what was going on in my heart. On the phone from California I had told her I simply needed to get away—that I was burdened about something, and needed a private place to think it through. She asked no questions. Ultimately, as time passed, I did reveal the anguish of my heart to her and she provided tremendous sanctuary—just what I needed. But that *occurred only as I felt free to talk about it, never because she pried into my problem. I returned to California five days later feeling better and refreshed.*

Two years after that, Judy needed my sanctuary—a place to retreat and work through a problem she was facing. She came to California and spent several days with me, and returned home in much better spirits. I was so glad that I could reciprocate in kind for Judy—a friend who had harbored me earlier when I was being buffeted by difficulty.

Judy is a friend par excellence. She is utterly devoted to those she loves. She is a correspondent without parallel and one who never forgets her friends' important dates and occasions. Her gifts are always clever, especially chosen to befit the recipient. When I moved from Dallas, she gave an open house for me, with the encouragement to "invite everybody in the City you want to say good-bye to."

She is a quality person in every area of her life, and it is impossible to outdo her. She seems to thrive on being available and generous with her time and energy. As I have been in the throes of writing this book, for instance, not one week has passed that I've not received a letter from Judy full of encouragement about this creative venture of mine. She takes time from the rearing of two children, the demands of teaching school, and all that is involved in her own personal life because she cares. It's as though she is constantly searching for new and interesting ways to reciprocate in the friendship. Everyone should have a friend like Judy.

The reason I list reciprocity as a priority is that it's impossible to have friendship without it. You may have associates or acquaintances, but you don't have friendship. Remember high school or college days when you made friends with your classmates and determined you would keep up with one another for life? Then you graduated and moved on? One of you wrote or called or gave and the other never reciprocated. What happened? That's right: The relationship died.

Friendship has to be reciprocal—a give and take arrangement of nurturing and growing together. It takes commitment. Investment. Time. Lasting friendship requires a genuine interest in the other person. It can rarely be one-sided and live; at least I have never had that happen in my experience. I don't forget those people who don't keep up with my life, but my energies don't gravitate toward them. A Christmas card occasionally, or a phone call here and there seem to suffice.

I'm not necessarily criticizing lack of reciprocity; obviously we cannot be close friends with everyone we meet, nor do we want to. But I am saying, if the friendship is very deep or lasts any length of time, it will be characterized by a mutual give and take over the long haul. At times the giving will also need to be sacrificial.

It's so easy to be selfish in friendship—to want things to go our way or be on our terms. I can be extremely selfish when it comes to investment of my time, energy, or money. I can think of my own interests or welfare or happiness and strive toward the goal of self-gratification. But in the end I'm never as content with the results as I am when I have given myself unselfishly to a friend. Why don't I do that more? Maybe I need to heed my example.

Judy was my instructor in Italian. Perhaps she can instruct me in unselfishness, too.

Freedom

Another priority that I seek in friendship is that of freedom. The freedom to which I refer has, in my mind, two meanings. First, a relationship will not have room to grow if there is not space given to each party—space to be one's own person and have autonomy—space to be free. While friendship is certainly a unified and unifying kinship, it is not a marriage. Sometimes we who are inclined to feel deeply about our friends forget that. We want to possess them. Possession in friendship will stifle the love and respect for one another quicker than anything else. It will ultimately kill relationships. This is an area in my life where I have had to do a lot of soul-searching work. I can be possessive with my friends and, although I am not proud of that fact, I have to admit it's the truth. I have improved in that area of weakness, but not before I hurt some people I loved. That I deeply regret.

When we hold back our friends, manipulating them to forego other relationships and opportunities for fear of losing them or losing our position in their lives, we do them a great disservice. We keep them from growing. This can be done very subtly, and once we begin that habit, it's hard to break. Therefore, I list freedom as an important ingredient in friendship development, because without it, there is the very real possibility that the friendship will not endure.

The second aspect of freedom which I feel is important in a relationship is somewhat harder to define. Being one who hates to give up on anything, I have always considered it anathema to let go of a friendship that was at one time so valued. That seemed hopeless, somehow. Nevertheless, I believe now that it is, in certain circumstances, the best way to handle relationships that are marked more by *pain than joy.*

For several years I have attempted to work through a major difficulty with a friend of mine. Early in our relationship we experienced harmony and great reciprocity, but with the passing of time a major area of conflict emerged. The conflict has existed and does exist to this day. We never fight and we don't even argue, but neither do we seem to be able to resolve the problem between us. It appears to be something beyond our control or regulation. We've talked about it at length, and prayed together about this difficulty specifically, but there remains a definite barrier that prohibits our unity. When we are together, the spirit of friendship suffers and we find ourselves tense and unnatural. At times in the past we have played "social games" in order to have the pretense of oneness and harmony, knowing that we were not being real.

It is a very unfortunate situation and something over which we have both agonized enormously. We find ourselves bewildered over this strange turn in what was once such a good relationship. After much reflection, deliberation, and prayer, I have finally concluded that the best approach to dealing with the dilemma is to let go of it. Let it be free from my mental and emotional quest for closure. Quit trying. If in the future the breach between us is healed, I will be extremely grateful; if not, however, I will no longer berate myself for an inability to change what seems to be inevitable: incompatibility in friendship.

I do not believe one's calling in friendship is to insist that everything be perfect before one can be friends with another, but neither do I think one should try to keep something alive under continual pressure. If friendship doesn't grow naturally and mutually, it doesn't grow at all.

Kindness

Everyone has a favorite quality that they look for in other people—that ingredient which captures their attention first. Some people look for strength as the basic qualifier for friendship. Others look for intelligence or humor or talent. I've known people to base friendships on good looks or an appealing body. But for me, the quality I am drawn to first and foremost is kindness.

I've tried to analyze the reason for that and the only satisfying answer I can come up with is that kindness in a person makes me relax—feel comfortable. It reduces any insecurities or preconceived fears I might have had upon first meeting. My father was the kindest person I've ever known and it reminds me of being with him, which I always enjoyed. The priority of kindness is simply a personal prerequisite of mine. I could never be close friends with someone who was not kind to me.

Mutuality

Our best friends are usually those with whom we have the most in common—the individuals who enjoy doing what we enjoy. The more we can do together, the more fun we have, and the more we learn.

I am a great one for projects and as far back as I can remember, I have been an adventuresome do-it-yourselfer. I've built rafts, rubber guns, wagons, cabinets, bookcases, desks, planters, wine racks, picture frames, lamps, and chess sets. I've repaired clogged sinks, running toilets, stuck shower stall doors, stopped clocks, dead radios, broken dishes, and defective hearing aids. I've tackled projects alone and used my feet, hands, toes, head, and teeth at the same time in order to get the job done. I've papered

walls, refinished furniture, china painted my own
dishes, made greeting cards, created wrapping paper,
woven rugs and pillows, macraméd wall hangings,
and designed and crafted a belt and matching pair
of shoes. And I have loved every minute of each one
of those projects.

Just about the time I thought I was becoming a
pro in some of these areas, I met Kurt. Ah, my friend
and incomparable companion, Kurt Ratican.
Actually, you were introduced to Kurt earlier. We
had Christmas together in May. There is hardly
anything Kurt cannot do—and do well. We had not
known each other a year before he taught me how to
silk screen. That Christmas I made all my Christmas
cards in the silk screen medium, under Kurt's patient
supervision. Then, for fourteen consecutive years I
repeated the project from the skills he had taught
me.

Kurt is the finest gourmet cook I know. His skill
in the kitchen and with creative recipes could rival a
French chef. On countless occasions we have cooked
together, making everything from pasta to an
enormous cake in the shape of Saint Peter's for a
welcome home party of friends returning from Rome.
Almost every valuable skill in the culinary arts I have
learned from Kurt.

My loom was a gift from him. He taught me to
weave and to dress the loom properly and how to
order yarns. He introduced me to certain patterns
that make weaving the most interesting or delicate
or beautiful. We have spent hours at his floor loom
making pillows, throws, rugs, bookmarks, guitar
straps, wall hangings . . . and cleaning up "bird nests"
as well!

When I have any problem with my plants, bulbs,
or flowers, I call Kurt. After I have explained the

problem he advises me on how to correct it and what
to do in the future.

Kurt is a phenomenal friend. Totally unique. I
feel we have almost grown up together, having known
one another for eighteen years. We used to talk about
getting married but we decided marriage would ruin
a beautiful friendship. Kurt said to me once, "Luci, if
we marry, you can make all the minor decisions like
where to send the children to school, and I'll make
all the major decisions, like where to plant lilacs in
the spring." Had I ever married I am certain it would
have been to Kurt, but the desire to be married was
never strong enough in either of us. The friendship
we have nourished through the years, however, is
definitely like no other.

Kurt majored in art during his college days and
our mutual love of art was a common denominator
from the beginning of our relationship. He has
traveled extensively, visiting every major continent
except Antarctica and, for a period of time, he lived
in Europe. He is the best-read individual in my
acquaintance and his library would probably make
two of mine. He tells me that the majority of his books
are being left to me in his will, which prompts me to
teasingly inquire about the state of his health each
time we're together. What a collection! The first
editions and rare books alone would be the envy of
any bibliophile.

I love to be in his house (which he has built) and
especially in his study, lined with bookshelves,
browsing for hours. We have tea and talk as we pull
the volumes from the shelves, discussing them and
reminiscing on many subjects together. He has a
massive assemblage of poetry books and has written
beautiful poetry himself. In one of his hundreds of
letters to me, this one dated July 5, 1969, he enclosed

a poem he had written while aboard ship on one of his around-the-world jaunts. He had fallen in love with the sea.

> Endlessly rising
> Out of the sea,
> Rising and falling
> And calling to me.
> Great rolling crags
> Purple and gold,
> Dusted with colors
> Subtle and bold.
> Here's my soul's home
> Ever to please,
> Close to the heavens,
> Close to the seas.

Who could not love a person like this, with such a sensitive soul and creative mind? Kurt's touch upon my life has expanded my horizons immeasurably. His patience and encouragement have made me attempt challenges I never dreamed possible; and in time I have, more often than not, seen them come to fruition. We love to do so many of the same things: listen to hours of music, discuss opera, plan parties, take pictures, fly kites, relive old times, dream dreams, try new things, build castles in the sky—plus all that I have mentioned before . . . and much more. In fact, I spent Christmas with Kurt last year and his gift to me was hot air ballooning over the Napa Valley . . . a first for both of us. To our disappointment the fog and rain forced us to scratch the plan, but not without making a reservation for this spring. Can't wait!

Kurt has given me many things that I cherish. I can look in every room of my house and there is something of his choosing or making. But of all his *gifts, this is the most treasured, given to me on my birthday fifteen years ago:*

Sonnet for Luci

Let me be to you as sunlight is
to a gently rolling hill,
Let me be to you as moonlight is
to waves that rise and spill.
Let me be to you as fleecy clouds are
to a summer sky,
Let me be to you as autumn breezes are
to fields gone dry.
Let me be to you as starlight is
to newly fallen snow,
Let me be to you as dawn is
to a bird song, soft and low.
Let me tell you how I love you,
Let me tell you so you'll know.

Hmmm . . . Now that I read that poem again, maybe marriage wouldn't ruin our friendship.

In this chapter you have been introduced not only to my prerequisites for successful in-depth relationships with others, but in a synthesized way, you've met four of my dearest friends: Marilyn, Kurt, Judy, and Sophia.

I treasure friendships and I look forward to continuing theirs and others for the rest of my life— growing, tracking, reciprocating, yet always encouraging my friends to be themselves. Additionally, I anticipate making new friends, ever widening my circumference of outreach and acceptance.

Be good to your friends! Give them your time and interest. Listen to their problems. Enter into their joys. Work through your difficulties in every way possible.

Be faithful and involved. Then, to celebrate this wonderful gift from God, take them to dinner. I know just the place to go. There's this nice little restaurant in Palm Springs . . .

Part Four

CASH–
Looking Ahead

Chapter Ten — Career

I have just had the best laugh! I picked up the morning newspaper to scan while I was having coffee and eating breakfast, and my eye caught an article entitled, "5.9 Quake Rumbles Through Eastern Canada, New England." Since I know people in New England I decided to read the article. It was an account of a sharp earthquake that shook the area, rattling dishes and shaking furniture as far south as Connecticut—the most significant quake in eastern Canada in more than a century. (That wasn't the funny part. I don't want you to think my sense of humor is that warped.)

As I read on, the things that I found humorous in the article were the names of the people involved; I mean, their names as related to their roles in the story. For instance, the geophysicist making comments on the size of the quake, from the U. S. Geological Survey in Golden, Colorado, was a man named Waverly Person. (An amusing name I have seen in the paper before, associated with earthquake news. Poor man. What other profession could he have chosen that would better befit his name?) The second notable in this drama reportedly said that the quake "sounded something like an airplane but the vibration *was greater—it was really shaking the house." She was a fifty-five-year-old woman named Marion Pray, which I'm sure she was doing at the time. (It's funny how, on certain occasions in life, last names change from nouns to verbs.) Then, the third individual who was quoted as saying, "The whole house was shaking . . . swaying from one side to the other," was Mrs. George Coffin.*

The reason I was tickled was that I realized one could almost follow the plot of the article by reading the names of the characters. Fortunately, Mrs. Coffin didn't die. I'm happy to report there were no injuries.

Then I thought about my own name and the numerous ways it has been mutilated. So many disparaging things can be done with the name Swindoll, and as far as I know, they've all been done. The most prevalent mutation, however, is Swindle instead of Swindoll. Now imagine, if you will, the connotations associated with one's profession stemming from <u>that</u> name, were it to become a verb! (For one thing, my brothers could never have gone into the ministry.)

Ironically enough, the first career I ever considered in my life was crime. Honestly! It was a short-lived vocation (less than twelve hours), but a real one, nevertheless. It started like this . . .

I had wandered into a grocery store to buy notebook paper on my way home from school one day, and while there I stole a package of cookies . . . six of those thin wafer type, with soft goo in the middle. I slipped them into my purse, surreptitiously, planning to eat and enjoy them as I walked home.

Eat—yes. Enjoy—no! With the first swallow I felt bad. No fault of the cookies; they were as delicious as any strongly desired junk food can be. I ate faster, thinking that would aid my digestion. The faster I ate, the faster I walked, but the sicker I got. By the time I arrived home, all six of the cookies were eaten and I was totally nauseated. I couldn't understand it. When my mother had made cookies I could eat six or more in one sitting with no problem and little aftereffect. (Remember the Hershey bars?) What was wrong with me?

The difficulty, of course, lay not in the consumption of the cookies, but in the stealing of them. I had been taught better. I even had the Spirit of God living within me at that time, having invited Christ into my heart when I was younger. It was as though my regenerate spirit refused to grant permission to my body to enjoy those cookies. Knowing they were stolen, my spirit bounded to its feet to do battle with my flesh. I was very young at the time (maybe nine or ten), and completely inexperienced about life; but that sickness became a spiritual touchstone for me much later as I sought to comprehend other battles in my life between spirit and flesh. I have never forgotten that feeling or experience.

When I got home, I walked right into the kitchen where my mother was standing at the sink, peeling potatoes in preparation for dinner. Her back was to me. Without a moment's hesitation, I exclaimed in one rapid-fire sentence,

> Mother, I stole a package of cookies on
> the way home from school today I don't know
> why I did it but I did I've eaten all of them
> and I feel sick I think I might die.

(As I said earlier, I've always had a flair for theatrics.) I talked very fast, thinking if I could get the story out in a hurry, I would be exonerated from my guilt quickly, and then I would feel better. But it wasn't quite that simple.

Mother put down the potato she was peeling and turned to face me. Although she looked surprised and was obviously disappointed in my behavior, she didn't spank me, nor did she lecture me. Many times, as I have reflected upon this happening in my childhood, I've realized how very wise she was in her discipline of me. She looked straight at me. The evening sun was streaming in through the kitchen window, falling on her face, making it appear as though it were bathed in a holy light. I can see her now in my mind's eye—like it were happening for the first time. She said softly, "Well . . . let's talk about this for a minute." Then she was quiet, thinking, but still looking at me.

> You know you've done something wrong and you've now got to make it right. You've eaten the cookies so you can't return them to the store, but you can tell the manager of the store what you did and pay for them. I think you'd better get your money and let's go do that now.

"Go back to that store? Oh, mother, I can't. I can't go back in there. What will they think of me? I'll die for sure then. Please! I can't do it." I was crying.

My mother absolutely would not take "no" for an answer. All the while I was making tearful excuses, she was gathering up her purse and car keys and walking toward the door. There was no waiting. Very reluctantly I got into the car, and before I knew it, I was standing alone in front of the store manager. Continuing to cry, I poured out my story of crime to him, telling him I was really sorry I had taken his cookies and I wanted to pay for them. My mother waited for me at the front door of the store.

He didn't say much, but he held out his hand and received the sixteen cents that covered the monetary cost of that escapade. At that moment, something interesting took place inside me: When the words of confession left my mouth and the coins rested in his palm, somehow my body felt better. The knots in my stomach began to untie themselves. As I walked away, toward my mother, she looked different to me; everything was different. I felt free, relaxed, clean—right. On the way home I thanked Mother for what she had made me do, and I don't know that I ever loved her more than I did at that moment. I said, "You know, Mother . . . I'm hungry." We both laughed.

No, a career of crime was never going to be my calling. I might have the name for it, but I didn't have the stamina.

Career development and preparation is another arena in which much has been written—similar to the subject of health in Chapter 4. There is a plethora of information available to the interested reader. On my own bookshelves I can count nine volumes relating to the secrets of success in one's career, all of which I have read at one time or another. It is a topic of great importance and concern for many people. The highly successful individual always evokes curiosity. We wonder how he or she did it. Often, we want to emulate the skills or style of their development in our own efforts to be successful. In fact, when anyone does anything with competency or aplomb, we take notice. This is nothing new. Michelangelo felt the same way in the 1500s.

Whenever I see someone who possesses some virtue, who displays some agility of mind, who knows how to do or say something

*more suavely than the rest, I am constrained
to fall in love with him . . .*[1]

The successful, qualified person always has a
following.

Naturally, in any level of success there are
personal secrets on how to get there. Everybody has
a formula that suits his or her personality and
temperament best. No matter what we read of these
formulas, however, or the degree to which we absorb
the "how-tos" for a successful career, we must still
develop our own plan.

The majority of questions that have been
addressed to me regarding my life as a single person
have, more often than not, pertained in some measure
to the issue of my career. Questions like:

1. How did you get started in what you do?
2. Did you have a career in mind when you
   went to college? Is your degree
   related to what you now do?
3. What is it like to experience success as a
   woman in a job that is primarily dominated
   by men?
4. Do you plan to stay with your present
   company until you retire?
5. Is it hard to uphold Christian principles in the
   business world?
6. Have you ever had to lower your standards to
   get where you are in business?
7. You must be rich—a single person who makes
   a big salary and works for an oil company . . .
   are you? (Generally asked by people under
   the age of sixteen.)

All of these are good questions . . . (all but number
seven, I mean. I usually answer that one with, "Wait

until you're my age, then time will have told you what you want to know.") and each of them has an answer. But rather than attempt to respond to specific queries, let me take another approach. I'll acquaint you briefly with my career, and then give you my three-part plan for maintaining it. From there, you make your own judgment and plans on career development.

I am employed by Mobil Oil Corporation, having worked for them since August, 1958. I received a college degree in commercial art in 1955 and went to work for Mobil as a junior draftsman in Research. Throughout the first eighteen years of my employment, I had several job classifications—senior draftsman, draftsman-artist, technical illustrator, and engineering draftsman. I worked in the field of Research until I transferred to the West Coast, entering the Pipeline Division of Mobil. (I related part of that story to you at the end of Chapter 3.) In 1976 I was promoted to the Rights of Way and Claims Department as an agent, representing Mobil in various activities. There are presently three of us in that department: my supervisor, a man; my colleague, a woman; and myself.

The work primarily encompasses four disciplines: law, negotiation, engineering, and appraisal. (Doesn't everyone who gets a degree in Commercial Art go into this field?) A Rights of Way and Claims agent with Mobil Pipeline acquires legal permission to occupy and utilize land for pipeline installation in both public and private sectors, and the footwork connected with the job is based upon that. The "Claims" part of the department, on the other hand, is associated with settling disputes related to problem areas which might arise in this type of occupation, as well as ascertaining data for damage reports. I *work in an office as well as in the field, traveling throughout the vicinity of Los Angeles and other parts of the state of California. Without any more detail, that's it in a nutshell! It is a challenging, interesting profession and one that I enjoy a great deal.*

Now, you may be thinking, "Luci calls that success? Why that sounds like the world's dullest job." And, for you, that's exactly what it might be: dull. Perhaps you wouldn't be suited for it. You'd be bored or find it too easy or too difficult. Or you could think it sounds like the ideal situation in which to work. In any event, the important criteria to consider in a career is whether or not we are suited for it and are able to accomplish our desired goals.

We should never try to transfer our own value judgments onto someone else's choice for a career. What might be extremely exciting or challenging to you could be utterly uninteresting to me, or vice versa. Anyway, being a Rights of Way and Claims agent may not be my Mobil job forever. I would like to believe that my performance will continue to improve year after year, resulting in even more challenging responsibilities being entrusted to me in the future. Of course, that won't be the case unless I do my present job well.

That brings me to my career fundamentals. Many years ago I heard a clever comment made on what it takes to move ahead in a career. I liked the comment and, in time, adopted it as my own. Having a successful career depends on three things:

> *—What you know*
> *—Who you know*
> *—What you know on Who*

What You Know

Knowledge is a tool. It enables us to accomplish tasks, fight battles, open doors, gain confidence, make decisions, and move ahead. It has no substitute. With this incomparable tool, we should be able to find our best niche in life and work efficiently and effectually there. Without it, the converse is true—we will "sit, soak, and sour." But not for long! In time we'll be replaced by someone who has the knowledge, or at least is willing to get it.

"A knowledge of what?" you ask. Here again, I would divide that into three parts. (Let's keep things in threes—they're easier to remember.) First, we need to know what to do! What occupation do we want to pursue in life, and what does it take to get there? It is quite possible we may not know the answer to this when we take our first steps down the road toward a career. That's why a liberal college education is good. Usually during that four-year period we will determine our career goals, if we have not already. College is not necessary for everyone of course, but some measure of schooling or education is imperative if we hope to move ahead in any field of endeavor.

When I first began as an agent for the Rights of Way and Claims Department, I knew very little about the disciplines involved—almost nothing, in fact, with the exception of engineering, which I had encountered as a draftsman. I began taking courses—some in night school, others through Mobil's educational programs, and still others by means of the International Rights of Way Association's offerings. They were extremely helpful and with the completion of each course, I became more confident about my work. Not only that, but the work became more enjoyable to me, and my job performance improved. So will yours. When we understand more fully what we're doing, anything is more enjoyable. As I've said before, there's nothing quite like accomplishing a task, and having a good time doing it.

Second, an extremely important area of "what you know" is <u>how to organize</u>. You've seen that little sign which reads, "A cluttered desk is the sign of a fertile mind." I find that amusing. but for me it is totally untrue. If my desk is unorganized for very long, I cannot get my work done. It may look like it was struck by a cyclone while I am working—papers scattered about, drawings on the floor, files on top of one another, books open, coffee cup handy, everything nearby—but when I finish the project, there is something in me that compels me to put things in order. I cannot function in chaos, and I never leave my office in the evenings with my desk in disarray.

This isn't true for everyone, however. When I worked for many years in the Research Laboratory, I was utterly amazed at how disorganized some of the most brilliant scientists could be. Almost fifty percent of the working force had their Ph.D.s, and some of them with the finest minds in America. But organized? No! I remember one of the scientists even had a little road map, which he jokingly distributed, of how to get around in his office. We used to giggle among ourselves at some of these brilliant, highly educated people; they could put a man on the moon, but they couldn't find their way to their desks. Obviously they were successful in their careers.

Some people can function best in the midst of clutter, but not everyone. If you are not accomplishing your work, are unable to locate quickly the items you need, and things around you are in turmoil, have a good housecleaning. Perhaps that will help.

Organization brings order out of chaos.

More important, learn to organize your time. You've heard it before, but it's true—everyone has the same amount of time, twenty-four hours. No one is different in that regard. The difference lies in how we spend that twenty-four hours. Make time work for you.

Last year I participated in two very fine seminars taught by Carol Sapin Gold, an internationally recognized management consultant. She is a specialist in time management and is president of her own firm in west Los Angeles. Here is a woman who gets things done! I thoroughly enjoyed those seminars and gained a great many new ideas in managing my own time. Carol is an award-winning author, a well-known speaker, and an excellent example of an extremely active, professional individual who coordinates a busy life with an ever-expanding career. If there are such seminars available in your area, it would behoove you to participate in one of them.

Third, a "trade secret" I have learned through the years in the area of knowledge is <u>when to stop</u>. People who are excited about their careers, who thrive on fulfilling the tasks that lie before them, thoroughly enjoying what they do, often do nothing but work. Workaholics! I have known a few, and not only are they boring individuals, but they are so wrapped up in themselves that they don't realize they fall into that category. Although I find a great deal of pleasure in my career and I definitely need to feel I am contributing to a meaningful cause, I cannot be classified as a workaholic.

I strongly advocate being a conscientious employee: Work hard, meet the challenge that lies before you, give your best and most energetic shot to the assignment at hand, strive toward better job performance. But work around the clock? Never. There are occasions in any profession where the demands are greater than the rewards, but if the job is so demanding that you have no home life, no church life, no play life, no love life—then be careful. Before you know it, you may have no life at all.

Here again is the need for compromise or balance. That is the key issue in any happy lifestyle—single or married. At times we have no choice about working late, arriving early, or sacrificing our own time to get a job done, but to live on that plane as the constant norm, simply because we can't say "no" (for whatever reasons), is a regrettable way to live. It's one of the more subtle forms of suicide.

Who You Know

In order to be effective in any career of your choosing, the first person you must know is <u>yourself</u>. What are your strengths? Weaknesses? Gifts? Liabilities? Where do your best talents lie? Are you a self-starter? Do you roll with the punches? Are you a leader or a follower? What are your methods in accomplishing goals?

On and on the questions go. What I am trying to say here is the better one knows one's self, the easier it is to determine one's calling in life. Make mental notes of your actions and responses to various task-oriented situations. They will aid you in determining how you work best. This activity is a never-ending process of knowing and growing.

I have a personal rule of thumb which I apply in getting my own goals accomplished. It is something I've learned by being consciously aware of my pattern and by repeating it purposely, in order to determine if it is generally true of me. It is true. And the knowledge of it has come from watching this pattern repeat itself. When I am faced with an abundance of work to be done, discouraged by the thought that I will never get out from under the load of it, I set a reasonable goal for myself, accomplish that end, do one more thing, then stop.

That may sound trite, or seem ridiculous, but the part that pushes me to hang in there is the "one more thing." That little bit of extra effort makes my mind think I'm working overtime. It's like an inner person saying to me, "You can do more, Luci. Go for it!" That one more thing may be to write a business letter, study an additional file, or make one last contact before I quit for the day; but whatever it is, it seems to help me over the hump of discouragement. Even though I haven't exceeded my goal by much, the fact that it's been exceeded at all makes me think I could do more if I had to. Then . . . I close up shop!

I learned to do this when I was in the Opera Chorus. There were numerous pages of music to memorize—in other languages—besides working at Mobil every day, and pressing rehearsal schedules every night. I would set a goal for myself of learning two pages, plus one more phrase, in my own rehearsal time. I sang at home, I sang at Mobil, I sang in the car, I sang in the shower—but each time I practiced or studied I would accomplish my goal and add one more "something" to it. Amazingly enough, before performance time, all the music was memorized. I accomplished what I wanted to; then I quit while I was ahead, with enough energy left to do something else.

The second individual you need to know is your supervisor. Make it a point to know his or her style. Is your boss an initiator or a responder, a listener or a talker, a stickler for detail or a happy-go-lucky individual? When you know that style, adapt to it to the degree that you can, while remaining true to your own person. Adapting to the personalities and working styles of people around you will aid toward team effort—a spirit which every office needs.

I remember my brother, Chuck, once referred to employee/employer relationships in a sermon of his, and the thing that has stuck in my mind was this concept: "Do you want to move up in your job? Make your boss look good—and do it genuinely." I would have to agree. There are occasions it may be difficult to do that, but there are many ways it can be done. And remember, in the meantime you are learning more about the job. You may feel at times you are given meaningless tasks to perform, but the more you know about what you're doing, the better off you will be in the future. Knowledge is your key to the future.

Knowing our <u>colleagues</u> is also extremely important. These are the individuals who stand in the gap, suffering and rejoicing (hopefully) with us through the trials and joys associated with the development of our careers.

In my present arena I could not be more fortunate. My fellow worker is a twenty-nine-year-old woman who has been employed by Mobil for eight years— Ruth Cronin. Ruth is very career-minded. She is responsible, teachable, intelligent, lots of fun—and single. We work harmoniously together and with enjoyable camaraderie. Prior to coming into our department last year she worked in Employee Relations, so she is acquainted with everyone in West Coast Pipe Lines, and by her outgoing personality, she is their friend.

I asked Ruth if she planned to remain with Mobil until retirement (a somewhat tenuous question for one so young and attractive as she . . . who has her whole life before her); but unhesitatingly she said, "Yes. I don't want to settle for less than the best, and I believe Mobil is the best!"

She has a desire to learn all she can about the career she is following, but not to the exclusion of her own personal dreams. I admire that. For example, she was offered opportunities to relocate in another branch of Mobil on a higher pay scale; but not wanting to leave Southern California, she refused. Since her teenage years she's known the direction she has wanted to go and has set her sights on that goal. There have been prices to pay in order to achieve it, but she has had the courage to pay them. With every rung of the ladder she has climbed, the reward at the top is nearer. Knowing her and working with her are among the reasons it's fun to go to work.

There have been other colleagues from my years of Research work who have served in my personal and career growth. In some cases, they began as office partners over twenty years ago but have continued to be some of my closest friends. They have supported me in my vocational development by their encouragement, even though we've lived miles apart, and their tenacity in friendship has always been a welcome mat when I have returned "home" for visits.

What You Know on Who

You have been eager to get to this page so you could find out who I have stepped on to climb the corporate ladder, right? Well, surprise! Nobody.

The "Who" of whom I speak is <u>God</u>, and what I know on Him is my most treasured knowledge. I know He is my partner in all ventures, going before me to straighten out the rough places before I get there. I know He is able to renew my strength when I am sick, weary, or tired of the daily grind. I know He will give me peace and hope when I'm worried or discouraged.

God won't make any mistakes with my life or my career. He has proven His faithfulness to His Word over and over and over. I know He loves me like no one else loves me, and He provides for me when no one else can. I know He has designed a future for me that, while it may not be easy, will always include His cushion of grace. What I know on God is the most valuable information I have in this life, and what He knows on me He'll keep to Himself. I know that, too.

A career is something to be proud of. Although it can be demanding, requiring continual structuring of our energies and time, it is extremely important for the single person living in the twentieth century. Over thirty years ago my father said to me,

> Honey, you can do anything you want in life, if you want it badly enough. It may take time and it will take hard work; but if you want it, you'll be willing to pay that price. It's up to you.

My father was right.

So . . . when I say to you, "You Can Do It," whatever it is—believe me, you can. I'm serious.

I might Swindle you out of a little package of cookies, but I'd never lie to you about a big thing like that!

[1]Robert J. Clements, *Michelangelo: A Self Portrait* (Englewood Cliffs, NJ: Prentice-Hall, Inc., 1963), p. 114.

Chapter Eleven Cash

If someone were to ask me the question, "Luci, what is your philosophy concerning money?" I would have to say it is a combination of two short comments I've read from two different women—both famous. One from our old friend Sophie Tucker, who said:

> I've been rich and I've been poor.
> And rich is definitely better.[1]

The other from Chanel, the French couturière:

> You don't need money.
> You need richness of heart, and elegance.[2]

Both are classic comments with truth in each one. But neither of them exactly captures my personal philosophy. I've never been rich so I can't truly identify with Ms. Tucker, but neither do I think having richness of heart and elegance is an adequate substitute for money. Don't get me wrong. I <u>certainly</u> believe in "richness of heart"—my philosophy of life is based in great measure on that premise—but there are occasions when that simply isn't enough. We do, at times, need money.

Therefore, I've combined the thoughts behind these two comments and have composed a little four-

line poem which would be my answer to the question
about my philosophy of money.

> Having money is better than not having
>   money,
>   I like the jingle of it in my purse.
> But if I trust money to buy a rich life,
>   Then the having of it is not a blessing;
>   it's a curse.

While money may be an important commodity to
have and while it may be impossible to get by without
it in the age in which we live, there are, of course,
many things that money cannot buy. It cannot buy
happiness or honor. It cannot buy strength of
character or good taste. Money can't buy wisdom. It
certainly can't redeem a soul that is alien to God.
While money does have a certain amount of power
and in some circles it does "talk," there are unlimited
things that it simply cannot purchase. Many of them
I've discussed in this book. Money can't buy
hospitality, kindness, a sense of humor, friendship,
good health, a love of the arts . . . things which
compose the "richness of heart" of which Chanel
speaks.

Therefore, with that qualifier in mind, as I discuss
money in this chapter—spending it, saving it, or
investing it—that discussion is on a plane completely
separate from the discussion of things which provide
"richness of heart." Since I believe it is impossible for
money to buy that particular quality of life, I put it
into a category of discussion all its own.

Spending

To say that a Christian does not need money in
order to function because he or she is of a higher
calling than this earth is sticking one's head in the

sand. We do need money—there's no doubt about
it—but what we need even more is the realization
that money is nothing more than a medium of
exchange, enabling us to do and have those things
we require or desire—things which money can buy. I
believe if we realistically view money as barter rather
than as an end in itself, we will be more inclined to
keep financial matters in proper perspective with the
whole of life. This view toward money takes some
conscious mental effort on our part but once the
principles for successful handling of finances are
established, put into practice, and continued,
financial equilibrium is virtually guaranteed.

I well remember my first lecture regarding money
and its value in life. I was ten years old and had
spent every penny of my allowance on model
airplanes. (I've always been fascinated by models of
all types—wood, plastic, cardboard. Four
Christmases ago, in fact, I bought the entire city of
Jerusalem in cardboard and built it into a tiny model
city . . . just for fun.)

In order to get the airplanes of my choice, I had
been eyeing the hobby store window for several
weeks, determining in my own mind which ones I
would buy when I had enough cash. I said nothing
to anyone. But I made silent plans in my head. When
I had accumulated seven dollars I went in the store
and bought three models, all the glue and dope I
needed (different "dope" than that of today, mind
you), two brushes, and a bottle of paint. If I recall
correctly, I borrowed an additional fifty cents from
one of my brothers in order to complete the purchase.
Then I took the bag of treasures home to show my
parents, thinking they would rejoice with me in what
I had bought.

When I set everything on the table, carefully

laying out each item, my mother said, "How much did all this cost?"

"Seven dollars and fifty cents. I had the seven dollars and Babe loaned me the fifty cents." (I've called Chuck "Babe" since childhood. A term of endearment for my younger brother.) I was smiling at her, hoping that would guarantee her approval of my astuteness in shopping. Instead, she shook her head, rolled her eyes, and walked away.

My father, on the other hand, very calmly asked, "Did you spend all of it on models . . . all the money you had?"

"Yes, Daddy. I did." The smile had left now. Then he said this, and I'll never forget it.

Buying models isn't a bad thing to do. Models are fun to make and you'll enjoy them, I'm sure. But spending everything you have on one purchase is bad. It's not wise to spend all your money on any one item. You see, it's the principle involved.

(He always said that when he lectured us on anything. It was hard for me to believe there were so many principles to living.) He continued,

Someday, when you're grown, you're going to be responsible for your own money. If you're careful with it—however you choose to use it—if you're careful, you'll always have money. Divide it up. Let it go in many different directions. Save some. Spend some. But don't put it all in the same place. I hope these models will mean as much to you as you think they will, because that's what you have now in place of your money.

Wise counsel from my loving father.

Of course, I have no idea where those models are; gone the way of all childhood treasures, I suppose. But my father's words have remained with me for forty years, and I've learned he was right about the principle involved. So often now, after I have purchased something, a small voice inside me says, ". . . that's what you have now in place of your money."

When I want to buy something, I determine in my mind if I want it more than I want the money in my pocket. If so, then I buy it. It's much like losing weight, I have found. If I want to eat something during the period of time I have set aside to diet, and that something is worth spending the calories on, then I spend them and try not to look back in regret. Life is full of choices and making a choice about spending money is up to me. It is my responsibility to do it carefully because no one else will do it for me. Nor should they. As a single, employed, responsible adult I should be able to determine what I want or need "in place of my money." That has become, more or less, my principle for spending.

Saving

Keeping in mind the fact that the successful manager of finances has money going in many different directions, I heartily recommend a savings program as one of those avenues. Not hoarding it, but systematically setting a certain amount aside for future use. This is not investing toward retirement. This is saving over a period of time for something we want or need which is considerably more expensive than one or two paychecks can cover. It is short-term, goal-oriented savings, if you will, usually with a specific date or item in view.

The first time I went to Europe for vacation was

*1966. I had dreamed of such a trip all my life but
never put much hope in those dreams because I
couldn't see my way clear, financially. In 1961 a
friend of mine and I began living in an apartment
together, sharing expenses, and she too wanted to go
to Europe. In fact, Charlotte (my roommate) had
relatives in Germany with whom we could stay, were
we ever to go to Berlin.*

*Charlotte and I talked very seriously of such a
trip together, and she suggested if I could save twenty-
five dollars a month for five years, in that length of
time I would have enough money to make my dream
come true. Being goal-oriented anyway, I thought
the idea sounded great. I wrote a letter to my bank
asking them to draft a twenty-five dollar monthly
withdrawal from my account; so it became an amount
of money I never saw. But I knew it was somewhere
in the bank adding up for Europe.*

*Occasionally during that five-year period, people
would say to me, "Gee, Luci, by the time you go you're
going to be so sick of saving, the trip won't be any
fun." Nothing could have been further from the truth.
I loved those months of aiming toward that goal,
knowing my twenty-five dollar deposits were
mounting up month after month.*

*During those many months of waiting for the
account to grow, I read and studied about Europe—
various cities we would be visiting, their museums,
cathedrals, and restaurants. Charlotte and I attended
travel programs together to enhance our knowledge
of the Continent. She bought an expensive camera
and became proficient with its intricacies and f-stops.
We talked about our trip often, planning it to the last
detail.*

*Then the year we had set for our departure came.
That was a very exciting time. Not only had I saved*

enough money to buy my plane ticket and secure
hotel accommodations, but I had enough left to join
Charlotte in inviting her sister, Ruth, to accompany
us on the trip as our guest. Ruth, like myself, had
never been abroad but had always wanted to go.
Charlotte and I were thrilled to be able to include
her financially in our plans, and it meant the world
to her. When we did get to Berlin you can imagine
the wonderful visit we had with their relatives.

In 1976, Ruth died very suddenly and
unexpectedly, but prior to her death she totally paid
back each of us for the money we had invested in
her trip ten years before, even though neither of us
ever once asked for it.

Had I never put that first twenty-five dollars in
my savings account, I would never have taken my
first trip to Europe. Since then I have gone four more
times, virtually by means of the same plan—putting
money aside monthly. The monthly amount for your
desired goal need not be big, but it must be consistent
to work. That has become, more or less, my principle
for saving.

Before we go any further, I have the feeling that
some of you are thinking, "Luci talks as if she has
always handled her money wisely as an adult. If
she has carefully followed her principles, then she
doesn't know what it is to be broke or be in debt or to
wonder if she'll make it, financially, to the end of
the month." My friends, if you are mistakenly thinking
that, then let me clear up the matter with the truth: I
have been broke. I have been head over heels in debt.
I have wondered how I would make it to the end of
the month. I have borrowed money. I have robbed
Peter to pay Paul, and I have made unwise
investments, thinking I would have more money in
the end, only to come out in the hole. I've done it all,

and I've done it as a responsible adult. So, please
don't think I am totally, moment by moment,
unquestionably solvent. No!

But I have learned some financial lessons the
hard way, and that is why I believe I can address
some of the money problems that a single person
must face. When I spell out my financial principles,
the reason I use the term "more or less" is that
principles are rules of right and best conduct, not
necessarily what we always do. They are measuring
sticks in determining our efforts to reach a desired
goal. However, money is money, no matter how you
slice it; and I do believe there needs to be a program
for the best management of it, whether or not we
follow that program to the letter.

Investing

Now, let's talk a few minutes about investments.
Investing money for future use is an important
financial responsibility for the single individual. The
reason for this is obvious. The unmarried person must
be concerned for his or her own future financial needs
because it is doubtful there will be anyone along the
way, standing in the wings, who is willing and ready
to meet those financial obligations for us. Planning
ahead in this regard, therefore, is essential. We must
strive to exercise control over our own financial
destiny, to the degree that we are able.

My advice in the category of being financially
successful for the future (primarily during retirement
years), is to seek guidance from someone who is adept
in the field of investment counseling—a financial
advisor or a trusted friend. This person should be
acquainted with the financial marketplace in terms
of what is best and what is available in planning
ahead for one's future. Mismanagement of money,

whether a lot or a little, can bring heartache and disappointment in our later years.

A wise advisor can look at your financial objectives in light of your resources and be able to set a realistic goal toward which you can aim for future solvency. It may sound difficult or involved but it really isn't . . . and it's extremely important.

From the first day I began working for Mobil in 1958, I started investing in the Mobil Savings Plan. I set aside a certain amount of my monthly salary to be used for the purchase of Mobil stock. That amount is met by a company contribution of five percent of my monthly income, which also goes toward stock purchase. When I retire, those joint savings in stock, coupled with my retirement benefits, will be the invested money on which I will live out my retirement years. Other investments I may have made through the years toward that goal will come to fruition then and will be added to that fund. If I am frugal and careful during my employment years I should have a comfortable retirement. That has become, more or less, my principle for investing.

The finest book I have ever read on handling money is entitled, Here's How to Succeed with Your Money, by George M. Bowman, a Christian author. The issues I have addressed in this chapter have been covered by him in that book, only in much greater detail. It is published by Moody Press and is written from a realistic, but biblical point of view. I have referred to it many times in my own financial planning and have found it trustworthy and beneficial in keeping me "on track." If you're having money problems you might pick up a copy and read it. I believe it could help in guiding your thinking.

Giving

The final area regarding the use of money is in giving it away. Generally, I believe we can truthfully say the happiest people we know, financially speaking, are those who are not afraid to give. They're the first ones to pitch in for a project that costs money; they often pick up the tab at meals; they send flowers when they don't need to; they buy greeting cards for everybody they know and mail them at appropriate intervals; they give more than a tithe to their church; they bring something to add to your dinner party; when they go on a trip, they always bring home a surprise, just for you; they bake cakes and bring them to the office or the classroom or to the board meeting. Givers . . . in every sense of the word! They are wonderful people to know.

One of the most generous individuals in my acquaintance, a genuine giver, is Bobbie Sharer. Bobbie is about my age and the mother of three boys. While her life has not been characterized by ease, it has been characterized by sacrificial giving. Actually, I do not know Bobbie well, having only been with her on a few occasions with her sister, Mary Graham, who is a personal friend of mine. I referred to Mary in Chapter 6 as one of the women who had fifteen lunch guests the day she and Ney Bailey moved into their new house. What I didn't tell you then was that Bobbie gave them that house. It is beautiful, modern, large, fully equipped . . . and paid for. She bought it for them! Through the years, Bobbie has consistently contributed financial support to Mary's Campus Crusade ministry; and if I visit in their home and comment on something new or different, the response almost always is, "Oh yes, Bobbie gave that to us." In Crusade circles she has been named, "Diamond Jim Bobbie," and I can certainly understand why.

When I had surgery two years ago and spent eight
weeks recuperating, there arrived at my house one
day in the mail a box of Godiva Cordials—from Bobbie
. . . because she knew those were my favorite
chocolates.

As I have thought about Bobbie and her gracious
way of giving to others, I've often been reminded of
Luke 6:38, where the Lord was speaking to His
disciples and the crowd of people who had gathered
to hear Him, encouraging them to live unselfishly.
He said,

> Give, and it will be given to you; good
> measure, pressed down, shaken together,
> running over, they will pour into your lap. For
> by your standard of measure it will be
> measured to you in return.

I am sure Bobbie is constantly being rewarded
for her generosity to others. She probably has had a
stack of treasures come her way, which she has in
turn passed on to someone else.

In closing, there is an area of giving money which
we have not yet touched upon, and we must. It is
the broad area of God's gifts to His children. No doubt,
each of us who knows Him personally has
experienced in some measure an unexpected
financial provision from our Heavenly Father. There
have been occasions when we have been without
faith or hope, but we witnessed God's providing for
our need because He is always faithful. He has
promised in Philippians 4:19 that not only will he
supply our needs, but that supply will come out of
His riches in glory in Christ Jesus. No bank account
in the world can match that Source.

God is utterly faithful to His children, whether
they are married, divorced, single, or widowed. He

loves us and He is in the business of demonstrating that love to us by providing for us. My favorite aspect of God's character is His ability to do things like no one else . . . with uniqueness, with His own flair, with His touch of class!

As we make our financial plans, therefore, for our present and future needs, let's never forget His ability to surprise us. We must leave room in our thinking and planning for His gracious, unexpected provisions. All He asks is that we keep our eyes on Him, rather than on our finances.

> Let your character be free from the love of money, being content with what you have; for He Himself has said, "I will never desert you, nor will I ever forsake you."   Hebrews 13:5

Wise counsel from our loving Father.

[1]Dottie Walters, *Success Secrets* (Glendora, CA: Royal CBS Publishing, 1978), p. 26.

[2]Rosalind Russell and Chris Chase, *Life Is a Banquet* (New York: Random House, 1977), p. 183.

Chapter Twelve—Conclusion

When I was growing up within my nucleus family—my parents, two brothers, and myself—we often spent Dad's two-week vacation period at my maternal grandfather's summer cottage. It was a rustic dwelling located near Palacios, Texas, on Carancahua Bay, but it had its own personality and beauty to us as a family. We had many wonderful times there.

With the exception of my older brother, Orville, all of us loved to fish and flounder. I think fishing bored him—hanging a line over the side of the boat, waiting an interminable amount of time (at least in his thinking) for something worthwhile to strike the bait. But he was not without his own amusement. He would sit on the bow of the boat, working miracles with a chemistry set while the rest of us caught the evening's meal. Chuck and I often wondered if Orville would invent something explosive during one of those fishing excursions and literally blow our ship out of the water. He had such a quick mind (still does, of course), and fishing was simply too slow for him. But the rest of us would loll about, chatting idly as the hours passed, informing one another when his or her cork would bob, insisting someone would surely "scare the fish away" from talking too loudly; and generally, as a family, we had enjoyable repartee. Thinking back upon those times now makes me smile. It seems I never had any problems or concerns during those vacations.

Going out there in the boat was an early morning activity, an entire family outing, but it wasn't the only fishing venture of the day. Quite often around 3:30 p.m., after we had all eaten lunch and rested, but while my parents were still sleeping, Chuck and I would sneak off with our poles and bait to the end of the pier. There we would continue our efforts to catch all the fish we could before the day was over.

We looked awful—T-shirts, cutoffs, ratty tennis shoes, baseball caps—but our hearts were light and carefree. Two happy-go-lucky kids on holiday! (I came across an old photograph the other day taken by someone who caught us sneaking out of the house. I looked at it carefully, wondering, "Who in the world is that? Good grief! It's us! Babe and me. We look like we've been hit by a fast-moving truck." Then the feeling of those occasions swept over me once again as I let my mind float back to our summer vacations.)

Here's what we'd do when we got to the pier: We'd set up shop—poles, bait, tackle box, empty bucket, candy bars—then we'd sit in the broiling sun, discussing the pros and cons of life, carefully watching for a strike and enjoying one another, except when we were arguing over who had caught the largest fish. You've wondered how Chuck learned so much about life and the scriptures? It was during these periods of time on the pier that I taught him everything he knows.

Into this scene of peace and idyllic surroundings there was only one ever-present, outstanding, uncontrollable blemish: another person. There was a man who always fished from the same pier we did, at the same time we did, but not in the same manner as we. His name was Mr. Kutasch (I suppose that's spelled correctly. I've never seen the name in print, except in my mind's eye).

"That Kutasch fella is an 'odd duck,' " my father used to say. We assumed by this that Daddy must have known more about him than we. Our only exposure to him was on the pier, but those experiences, in and of themselves, were certainly peculiar enough to earn him the label "odd." Mr. Kutasch always sat some distance away from us but in plain view. From where we sat we could, amazingly enough, watch him, his cork, our lines, and each other, all at the same time. Eventually, however, we realized the most important item to watch, by far, was his cork. With the slightest bobble of it, Kutasch would jerk that line out of the water so fast that had a fish been on it, the hook would have ripped out the side of its mouth . . . and, had it survived, it would certainly have gotten away.

During all our summers of fishing with Kutasch, never once did we see him catch a single living sea animal which made its habitat in Carancahua Bay. But it wasn't because he didn't try. The voracity with which he entered into that sport spoke of his enthusiasm. This thin, flailing, beast-of-a-fishing-line of his, with its untamed hook on the end, became a menace to the waterfront. When he engaged in this characteristic maneuver prompted by almost every cork wobble, all living creatures for blocks around hit the deck. The line wrapped itself around loose pier boards, the boathouse, crab nets, drying fish heads, buckets, camp stools, towels, and on one occasion, my nose!

We simply couldn't understand it. Here was a man who gave his all to the game of fishing, totally committed to catching whatever had caused the cork to bob, but not once being rewarded for his effort. We wondered why he never gave up. But he was always there—and consistently with the same behavior.

In time, we labeled this unusual custom of his, "givin' it the Kutasch." And when things got boring on our end of the pier, there was no activity in the water, or we simply wanted to demonstrate that we were still in the fight, one of us would say to the other to "give it the Kutasch," just to liven things up. That signified: "Watch out, you fish. I'm still here and I'm ready for you. In fact, I'm out to get all you've got!"

Even now, many, many years later, when Chuck or I face a new venture, a difficult challenge, or one of us is uncertain of the outcome of an undertaking, our words of encouragement to the other might very well be, "Give it the Kutasch." We are saying, in effect, "Go for broke! Don't hold back. You may not know what's out there, but whatever it is, give it your all." It says, "Watch out world . . . here comes enthusiasm!"

My dear, single friends—if I could close this book with one ringing message in your ears, it would be once again to encourage you to get into the enthusiasm of living. Don't wait for a mate. Don't wait for more time. Don't wait until you have more money. Don't wait until both your feet are on the ground. Don't wait for <u>anything else</u>. The time to be involved with living is now—not tomorrow or next week or next year. Now.

You say, "There are so many problems with being single. I'm lonely, I'm bored, I don't know how to enjoy things by myself." Of course there are problems. There are problems in any lifestyle, because that is part of the living process. One cannot take a hand axe and chop a narrow path through the jungle of problems that exist, and then say, "Here's the path . . . walk through here and your problems are over." No, that isn't realistic. But there are tremendous hopes and untold blessings in the midst of those problems.

I would venture to say many of your problems as a single person exist because you are holding back. You're waiting for something better to come along, that certain something that will enrich your circumstances. Well, friends—it's here. It's called Life. And Breath. And God. That's all you need. You don't have to be married to be happy. You just have to be alive.

God has wonderful things in store for us as singles when we let go and get involved with the richness and rhythm of life. I have spent the entire length of this book in an endeavor to underscore that truth. . . .

Hey! Your cork is bobbin'. The whole wide world is on the end of that line. Give it the Kutasch!

Bouquets

If thou of fortune be bereft
And in thy store there be but left
Two loaves, sell one and with the dole
Buy hyacinths to feed thy soul.[1]

I love flowers. I love receiving them and I love giving them away. They brighten the day for me, and when given or received, they convey many emotions.

Were the setting in the above poem my present state, and had I just purchased those hyacinths, I would give them all away "to feed the souls" of five very special people who have made this book possible. The bouquets would, of necessity, have to be small (money from one loaf won't buy many flowers), but they would be full of love and appreciation.

The first two bouquets of hyacinths would go to John Van Diest, Publisher, and Julie Cave, Managing Editor of Multnomah Press. On July 22, 1981, John talked with me about writing this book. Although he had known me only a few hours, he put a great deal of blind faith in a brand new author and he, along with his warm, friendly, competent staff, has verbally supported me for the past seven months of writing. Julie, whose voice I heard for the first time on December 9, 1981, and whose friendship is a joy to cultivate, has become a very real source of delight as well as loving encouragement. My sincere thanks to the entire Multnomah Press family. By your acceptance I feel I've become a part of it.

The next bouquet would, without doubt, be handed to my incomparable typist and delightful friend, Nancy King. Nancy's abilities at the typewriter keyboard have been utilized in this venture for so many consecutive weekends that she probably wonders if she still has a life of her own. I have called her at pre-dawn, high noon, and midnight to make an alteration on the manuscript, and never once has she gotten upset or shown the slightest sign of irritation. Her neatness, sense of organization, attention to detail, and dedication to this project have indicated repeatedly that I gave the right answer that day last summer when she asked, "May I type your book?" You have typed it, "Toots," and done an outstanding job. I thank you with all my heart and I give you these hyacinths to show my thanks. And not only flowers, but a thousand kudos as well! Or, would you prefer dinner at a nice restaurant? Oh no! <u>Not</u> Banducci's!

The fourth bouquet of flowers must, of course, go to the guy we all know and love, Chuck Swindoll. Babe not only began paving the way for this volume to go to press, by encouraging me to "unveil the mystery" and "open the vault" of my world, but his scriptural ministry has had, through the years, a profoundly positive effect upon my life and thinking. Perhaps without his realizing it, my philosophy of life is to some degree the product of his teaching and influence. He and my older brother, Orville, have *both touched my being, spiritually, to such an extent that there would never be enough flowers in all the world to express my thanks to them for that. By the way, I should confess: I really didn't teach Babe everything he knows while we sat on that pier as youngsters at Carancahua Bay—just some of the crazy brother/sister illustrations to which he so often refers in his sermons. I must admit, however, when I'm in church now or turn on my radio and hear him preaching, I shudder when he begins with, "My sister and I used to . . ."*

And finally, the fifth and last bouquet of flowers must be put in the hands of my closest confidante, Marilyn Meberg, the best listener I've ever known. She has heard these words and read these chapters from beginning to end. I have collared her on innumerable occasions to help me properly structure a sentence or paragraph. Together we have wrestled with the alphabet, a dictionary, a thesaurus, and each other, in an effort to form cohesive thoughts out of my life's experiences. Her input has been invaluable.

Once she was an articulate, well-balanced English professor, but with my repeated demands upon her time, energies, and mental abilities she succumbed to the inevitable strain. Now I'll have to take these flowers on one of my weekly visits to her . . . in a home for the mildly deranged.

[1]John Bartlett, *Familiar Quotations*, ed. Christopher Morley (Boston: Little, Brown and Company, 1951), p. 682.